Advance praise for **Your Finest Hour**

"*Your Finest Hour* is a comprehensive success manual that introduces you to a world of new possibilities. Dennis Haber provides inspirational guidance and action steps to help you maintain a positive focus, no matter what challenges may arise. If you want to achieve more, build solid relationships, and live life to the fullest, *Your Finest Hour* will show you the way."

—Jeff Keller, author of *Attitude is Everything*

"No matter how far you've gone on the wrong road, it's never too late to turn back. Dennis Haber's easy and fun read, *Your Finest Hour*, outlines the best way to do so. Perfect for every stage of life and life situation, it informs and educates. Be prepared for a better you!"

—Justice Marsha Steinhardt Feldman (Ret.),
New York State Supreme Court

"Stuck is not the worst place to be. But it is far worse to be moving in the wrong direction as you 'wing it.' To move in the right direction, it is important to access the concepts and strategies contained in *Your Finest Hour*. This book is an absolute must-read because it acts as your game of life NFL playbook. Dennis provides all the X's and O's, the plays, and the reasons for your next move. Now it's time to ask an important question: *How much will it cost me if I don't read this book?* The answer: *It will cost you a lot.*"

—Dr. Dan Schaefer, author of *Click! The Competitive Edge™ for Sports, Entertainment, and Business*

"*Your Finest Hour* is a transformative guide for anyone committed to breaking free from the status quo and focusing on achieving true success. Author Dennis Haber eloquently addresses many of the key points, strategies, and tactics to win in the game of life, success, family, and relationships. This book provides a holistic approach to personal and professional development and is a must-read for success-minded individuals ready to elevate their lives."

—**Rob Fishman**, author of *Retail Success in an Online World* and president, Sandler-Hauppauge Long Island NY

"Being an entrepreneur can be a lonely place. The long hours and constant stress of running a business had me close to defeat, as I was surrounded by imposter syndrome feelings. *Your Finest Hour* not only helped me break free from this mindset, but it also stopped me from living in fear. In his book, Dennis gave me the tools to reel my confidence back in so I could become the person and leader I wanted to be. If the concepts and strategies outlined here worked for me, they will work for you."

—**John Dunlop**, founder and CEO, Intent Athletics, Inc.

"I love that chapters end with a summary of Action Steps. Dennis Haber is able to distill his experience, pithy anecdotes, and the wisdom of others into an easy read. It was great to be reminded of so many life lessons and to consider new ones. *Your Finest Hour* is a great gift for any professional or student!"

—**Vikram Rajan**, cofounder, Practice Marketing, Inc.

"If I were looking for all the information I would need to break into the business world, *Your Finest Hour* would be my resource. It's a user's manual for how to look for, find, start, progress, master, and complete a career in virtually any field in today's marketplace—from personal habits to professional proficiency. Just amazingly thorough, complete—and doable!"

—**Laurie Magers**, executive assistant to Zig and Tom Ziglar

"This isn't just a book; it's a tool for real personal improvement, encouraging you to face challenges head-on and pursue your goals with persistence. Dennis offers practical advice on handling failures and building a growth mindset. The exercises made me think deeply about my life and choices, and the sections on self-talk emphasize the transformative impact of our inner dialogue on personal growth. A must-read for anyone looking to better themselves in a straightforward, effective way."

—**Jerry Allocca**, CEO, Connected Culture

"Dennis brings his unique perspective to the topic of self-awareness and lends an important perspective for all of us to consider and act upon. *Your Finest Hour* requires the reader to stop throughout the book to review earlier chapters that reinforce concepts used as building blocks for his educational process. This is a clever approach to enhance and simplify the author's impact of what is a complex subject matter. This book offers the potential for a life-changing experience for the reader. Few books open the doors for this type of opportunity."

—**Chase V. Magnuson**, coauthor of *The Secret Power Behind Real Estate Donations* and president, Real Estate for Charities

"How do we reverse course in our lives? Dennis Haber's latest book, *Your Finest Hour*, gives us all we need to know. None of us has time to linger if we want to walk a new path. Dennis provides exercises and questions that we are compelled to ponder and, yes, answer. It works! He also asks us to decide on what we want to be and to mirror (model) that image. The image materializes and becomes reality, and with time and work, we achieve our goals. This book can and will change your life. The practice of modeling transformed mine."

—**Beverly J. Bell**, attorney; author of *Whispers, a Novel for a New Millennium* and *Violet Sun*; and Ordained Minister of Word and Sacrament in the Reformed Church in America

"*Your Finest Hour* is a superb guide for taking your life to new heights of achievement. It contains a treasure-trove of ideas that debunks myths, interrogates stubborn beliefs, and offers new and refreshing perspectives about how to awaken your full potential. Dennis shares his timeless thoughts that will lead to a life well-lived in your business, family, and personal endeavors. It's your turn to become unstoppable.

—**Matthew Linderman**, CCM, president, COO, and general manager, Boca West Country Club

YOUR
FINEST
HOUR

Living Life at a Level
You Never Thought Possible

DENNIS HABER

DHCM MEDIA GROUP, INC.

Published by DHCM Media Group, Inc.

DHCM MEDIA GROUP, INC.

Produced by GMK Writing and Editing, Inc.
Managing Editor: Katie Benoit
Copyeditor: Amy Paradysz
Text design and composition: Libby Kingsbury
Cover design: Libby Kingsbury
Printed by IngramSpark

Print ISBN: 979-8-9893952-1-7
Ebook ISBN: 979-8-9893952-2-4

Visit the author at **dennis@dennishaber.com**

Your Finest Hour lets you grow into the champion you aspire to become and has your friends thinking *I too want to be like that.*

This book is dedicated to those wanting more out of life—a life that radiates joy, accomplishment, and respect—and who are ready to turn far-reaching and impactful ideas into life-changing results.

ACKNOWLEDGMENTS

Writing is a lonely, secretive, and personal endeavor. As thoughts become words, and words become cogent ideas, the mind, working overtime, also acts as a first line editor. Ideas cry out for recognition. Some must be given their rightly status; others turn out to be not quite as good as initially thought; while others are moved or are erased because they just don't make the grade. There is only so much an author can do. If you want a book's thoughts to sparkle, you need a team to come to the rescue.

My team made sure that happened: Amy Paradysz, Katie Benoit, and Gary Krebs challenged me to go deeper with my thoughts. They caused me to rethink and reframe ideas. Their collective literary and organization skills made this book into my finest hour. The cover and interior page design showcases the talents of Elizabeth (Libby) Kingsbury. Thank you all.

Shelley, my savior in life, read and reread chapters and gave me unvarnished advice—which I heeded. A special thanks to my boys, Jason and Cory, who always offer sage counsel and support.

A huge shout out to Beverly Bell, my friend since first grade, colleague, and fellow author, who read the very first draft of the book. I am grateful for your expertise and encouragement. I am also thankful to so many of my friends (you know who you are) who encourage and inspire me.

CONTENTS

Your Finest Hour invites you to relaunch and reclaim your life. These are the three superpowers you will gain from reading these pages:

- Your superpower of appropriate response.

- Your superpower of awareness.

- Your superpower of thought creation and thinking control.

AUTHOR'S NOTE

It is time to see the truth, speak the truth, and live the truth. Like so many people today, I had lived a part of my life in fear of the truth. This is no way to live.

It is difficult to be productive when your confidence is drowning in an ocean of sorrow and you don't have the tools to reel it in. But the principles, concepts, and ideas in *Your Finest Hour* came to my rescue and changed my life. It stopped me from playing and remaining the victim. It stopped me from blaming others where the blame was mine. It made me take a good look in that proverbial mirror of life. I longed to be better. I wished to be my own person. I needed to be the person I wanted to become.

Since my freshman year of college, I've read and listened to the great thinkers on human development. I've learned from their prodigious thoughts on the power of the mind. My teachers included the likes of Zig Ziglar, Dale Carnegie, Earl Nightingale, and Orison Swett Marden. The people, books, and tapes I culled wisdom from are too numerous to count.

Now I live in a world where learning is all that matters. I thrive in this world because I have nothing to fear, lose, or be defeated about. This is a special place where you, too, can spend all your time living, learning, and yearning.

The first thirteen chapters of this book cover the principles behind *Your Finest Hour* and what it feels like to live life in total mental freedom.

Mental barriers can be stubborn and difficult to detect. When they lead to habitual thinking and behavior, they can turn destructive, especially with relationships. Solving "simple" problems even becomes a challenge. Spiritual growth becomes tricky. Becoming society's dead weight is stigmatic and embarrassing. Now imagine this is you.

I know—and everyone who has been through the process of *Your Finest Hour* knows—that the inner world can be rescued and detoxed. In Part 2, Chapters 14–27, I show you how to get the most out of the process. In the Appendices, you will find inspiring communication ideas.

You will discover, as I have, that becoming self-aware is critical to navigating life. This process is also about taking corrective action to ameliorate the calamitous damage caused by your thoughts and actions. You'll learn how to flip the switch and activate *your superpowers of appropriate response, awareness, and thought creation and thinking control* at just the right times. They are also referred to as the three superpowers.

This book is filled with compelling ideas that can act as your personal training simulator. Like a pilot, you'll have the opportunity to recognize and "experience" events *as a practice*, so you are ready for "the real thing" when you encounter that situation in life. Your greatest danger is not understanding and noticing that your greatest danger is closer than you think.

Life is made up of a series of problems to moan about, do something about, or prevent from happening in the first place. The latter two is where you get to strut your stuff.

I have transformed my life by re-engaging with my internal self (we are best buddies!). And you can do the same. Watch how friends, family, and colleagues marvel at the *you* that you always wanted to be—and have now become.

—Dennis Haber
Boca Raton, FL

FOREWORD

Dennis Haber is living his finest hour. It didn't happen overnight Nor did it happen without overcoming all that life can throw at you. I am grateful that he has elected to share the principles and practices he has discovered and incorporated into his own life, because they are exactly what can be used by anyone seeking to grow to their finest hour. I particularly appreciate how clearly he states each concept and how specific he is in setting out the exact paths and steps to take for achievement.

Your Finest Hour is a handbook for anyone, no matter where you might be in your own life, establishing the processes required to create a foundation based on strength—of mind, of character, of faith, of competence, of self-confidence. It offers clear instruction on how to control your thinking and redirect your negative thoughts to positive ones. It emphasizes deliberate, continuous learning and explains the value of "hanging in" during difficult times.

I love how Dennis shows that success in any endeavor is possible—and even inevitable when you plan for it, prepare for it, and expect it. Dennis's presentation makes it all logical and his roadmap is doable, particularly because it comes from his personal experiences. Balanced, clear, positive, encouraging thinking combined with acceptance of appropriate personal responsibility can result in experiencing the value and joy associated with continuous learning. If you have an appetite for success, then feed your mind this book!

—**Tom Ziglar**, *CEO Zig Ziglar Corporation*

INTRODUCTION

YOUR CHANCE FOR GREATNESS

Your Finest Hour is about the unused existential power that lies dormant within you. By continuing to ignore this unused power, your potential for achievement will be vastly impaired. As your life remains unfulfilled, undeveloped, and incomplete, you will constantly revisit your weakened, stand-by query, "Is this all there is to life?" Refusing to tap into your impressive power will be the biggest mistake you will ever make.

The seeming unfairness and cruelty of life will follow you around like a shadow. You will believe that everyone else is happier than you, even though you have cause to be happy. Troublesome thoughts will keep piling on, as you imagine other people skating through life. But there you remain, stuck pulling life's heavy weights of disappointments, calamities, and setbacks.

At some point, you will have had a bellyful. Your mind will urge you to find a better way. When the point of ENOUGH has been reached, you will finally battle back with mental ammunition that will destroy everything that was destroying you. Your job is to let counter-thoughts get fully expressed so you can bravely fight back to rescue the life that is rightly yours.

There is a powerful, wonder-thought vying for attention. Imagine how your life would change if this thought instead followed you around like a shadow: *Every event that I experience provides me with the invaluable good fortune to learn, improve,*

4 YOUR FINEST HOUR

and get better. You will never ask that wobbly, fragile question, "Is this all there is to life?" ever again. You will start living your life the way you want to live your life. This book isn't about you becoming one of the most prodigious titans who ever lived. It's about honoring your life so you can become the best *you* who ever lived.

Think about it: "Every event that I experience provides me with the invaluable good fortune to learn, improve, and get better." This belief will lead you to life's riches. You will be happy, healthy, reasonably secure, maybe even prosperous, and have satisfying relationships with family, friends, and acquaintances. You will also have plenty of hope for the future for yourself and for your family.

Others have passed you by while you remained invisible to them. But there will come a great day, when you will then pass those who once did the same to you. You will rise high, as you master how to get the most respect, dignity, and esteem out of your business life, personal life, and family life.

My first book, *Don't Play with Fire: How to Keep Your Greatness from Going Up in Flames,* began with a foundational chapter entitled *Be in Learning Mode.* What can be accomplished without employing this fundamental principle? Without it, every other tool, strategy, and approach to life becomes ineffective. In this book, the words or phrases *learning, Learning Mode,* and *the Learning Mode Effect* are used interchangeably. Regardless of use, they represent a code of defining principles and truths that will profoundly change your life and challenge you to be, do, and have more than you ever thought possible.

In this book, I greatly expand upon the principle of Learning Mode and how to use it to change your life. Your new self will blaze a trail of success, as your old self watches in amazement. The goal here is to sharpen your mind as it has never been sharpened before. You will be tested in surprising and unexpected ways. Life will constantly implore you to show it "what you got."

You will triumph when that person, hidden deep within that secret place, finally emerges.

Now you can give birth to your true self, so you can live your finest hour. Your bravest moments, when you need to summon up courage, will never slip away again because of fear. Mastering the information in this book allows you to shape the interpretation of the stories of your life. Imagine what this will mean for you at work and at home.

Your Finest Hour is your personal guide that shows you how to squeeze the maximum out of the most important investment you will ever make—your investment in *you*.

Life becomes much easier to live when you make things go right rather than deal with things only after they go wrong. Your finest hour contingency planning allows you to correct mistakes more quickly.

Think of the times you gave in and gave up because you didn't want others to see your embarrassment of impending failure. *Your Finest Hour* provides you with a new way to look at failure. In essence, it is spelled o-p-p-o-r-t-u-n-i-t-y. Once you grasp this thought-provoking idea, you will understand how your misplaced confidence in your comfort zone constrained your efforts. Your comfort zone is actually a hidden danger zone.

Deleting the "F" words—failure and fear—from your functional vocabulary is quite easy when you have the courage to live beyond the boundaries of your comfort zone. The Learning Mode Effect provides the determination and courage you need to do what many don't, won't, or can't do—to dare to be better.

Your newfound power stems from becoming aware of life's patterns and contemplating corrective thoughts, implementing reimagined actions, and arranging curative care toward your important relationships. It shows you how to maximize those thoughts, actions, and relationships as you use life to build a better life.

You can become the "Superman" of your life. *Your Finest*

Hour destroys all the "I'm scared, I'm tired, and I'm afraid" kryptonite in your path. It's your turn to be "more powerful than a locomotive," to "leap tall buildings in a single bound" so you can produce your own impossible dreams that you can now make possible.

Reading the book is only the first step. Study it, internalize the concepts, and practice them often. What and how you think could greatly affect your life. The power for making your life phenomenal lies with you. You may be known for one good thing at work and at home. By next year, think what would happen once your skillsets and personal traits make it possible to be known for many more good things.

Never again will you be afraid of how much you do not know. Your greatness lies in learning something new, as you make this "do not know" gap smaller.

It is my hope that you will have quite a few ah-ha moments as you appreciate the extraordinary outcomes that can accompany *Your Finest Hour*. I want you to succeed today, win tomorrow, and prosper forever. And you can and will when you adopt this material as your own.

You can live your life any way that you want, but you get to live it only once. Get ready to have the greatest experience of your life. A whole new world is about to unfold. So, let's get going!

Part 1
Insights and Wisdom

CHAPTER 1

SETTING THE SCENE

Establishing deep and important relationships is a fundamental requirement if you are going to create your finest hour.

Life is hard. Wishing, hoping, and praying that life becomes much easier won't help at all. It is time you stop making it harder. In the time it took to read the last two sentences, thousands of people will regret the decisions they just made. Because of this, their lives will be in utter turmoil, as they confront the unconsidered dire consequences that will surely follow. Many will not be able to salvage much from the hardships and mishaps that will surely ensue.

But you will be able to do it better than most because you are about to discard the parts of life that caused you to live in fear. You will also develop the eyes of an eagle, as you will finally see things you couldn't see before. This will lead to much better decision making.

For a moment, let's pretend that you are magically transported to a time and place where you are the only person to inhabit the planet and can do what you want, believe what you wish, say whatever rolls off your tongue, and feel any way that you desire. Better still, you would never have to make concessions to others nor be concerned with the consequences of your acts. In this make-believe world, the mind would eventually wither and die because it would have no purpose. There would be no mental constraints and no need to build any human relationships.

Life Without Purpose

Were you to coexist along with plants and animals, as imagined, there would be no human interaction or time reference points. The past, present, and future would cease to exist. There would be no such thing as success or failure; enlightenment and ignorance wouldn't exist either. There would be no victim mindset. There would be no measurement to determine mental and spiritual growth.

Because, as above noted, typical mental metrics couldn't be used, life would be *sooooo* easy. Things would just be as they are. There would be no added back stories to clarify ambiguous or unambiguous situations. There would be no need for different perspectives, insights, and emotions, as human relationships would be non-existent. You would never have to dig deep to find your center core humanity.

Accordingly, you would never have to ask piercing existential questions of yourself. Life in addition to being *sooooo* easy, would also be *sooooo* boring and *sooooo* unsatisfying. Imagine a life where each day is a carbon copy of the day before. Each day would be lived effortlessly, without context and nuance.

Transporting yourself into this fanciful, make-believe time and place where you were the only human inhabitant illustrates that life can be lived to the fullest only in community with others. Yet, far too many people violate the rules of respectful coexistence. They follow the harmful practice of inertia and complacency. With the former, people continue to do what has worked in the past. With the latter, people ignore future risks. In the real world, when you focus only on you, relationships can become fleeting, troubled, or fade away completely. Life could be unnecessarily difficult. Here are some common examples we often face.

If you are a doctor, you walk out of the exam room to see the next patient just as your current patient asks a question. Your mission and purpose cannot be just how many patients you see in a day. What happened to the caring and concern for the patient?

If you are a contractor, you create inflated estimates by increasing your costs by a significant margin. You deliver inferior products to the construction sites. Your mission and purpose cannot be just about maximizing revenues on each project. What happened to the pride of giving the customer his dream home at a fair price?

If you are a gym proprietor, you order inferior equipment with bottom-rung maintenance contracts. Your mission and purpose cannot be just to skimp on equipment, while maximizing membership. What happened to the desire to help the clients feel good about themselves?

If you are a boss, you constantly upbraid your employees for the slightest infractions. Because they are afraid they will make a mistake, production falls to a crawl. Your mission and purpose cannot be to be an all-powerful executive who misuses authority. What happened to the original dream to be the finest company in the industry?

Wherever you are in life, you may long for more. For example, you may wish to erase your past, or correct recent harmful mistakes, or take advantage of improving your attitude and abilites for a chance to become the person you really want to be. Because these actions cause others to notice, they will be expecting even more from you, as they wonder how they too can improve like you have.

Are you the person who struggles to find customers or are you the person who has enough customers at the moment? Are you the individual who can't keep a friend, or are you the individual who knows how to be a friend and has them in abundance? Are you the person people ignore and treat with indifference when it comes to giving advice because you have nothing to offer, or are you the person people seek out for advice? No matter where you are in this continuum, you most likely will become a victim of inertia or complacency. Each will cause a multitude of problems. Each problem can be ameliorated through the process of the Learning Mode Effect.

BE SELF-AWARE

Live Effectively in Community

It has been shouted from the rooftop for hundreds of years that most of one's financial and relationship successes are not due to technical knowledge but due to an understanding of how to get the most out of human relationships. At a minimum, the effective way to accomplish this is by being genuine and credible. These two mindsets set you up for living a life that is well-lived. Along the way, you will also grasp both what to learn and how to learn.

That old Zig Ziglar thought becomes urgent: "People don't care how much you know until they know how much you care about them." This holds true in both your personal and business life.

The Error: The fundamentals of relationship building are ignored.

The Fix: There is no substitute for letting people know that you care about them.

The Learning Mode Mindset

Learning and the Learning Mode mindset has unlimited

potential. Reversing the fear of taking a step back as you seek to improve will become a new strength instead of a lingering weakness. Faithfully applying this principle could slingshot your life forward as your deepest hopes and dreams get confirmed. You will never be stopped from moving toward your desired goal again. You will have the determination to relaunch and, finally, reclaim your life, as you interact with others. You will begin seriously examining thoughts and actions that held sway over misapplied strategies that made the situation worse, certainly not better. Your feet will no longer be encased in cement where forward progress is unmercifully halted. You can leave behind the old model of believing things only after first seeing them—and begin seeing what you believe. With this shift, you can create your own future.

Make Life Exciting and Meaningful

While you can live your life any way that you choose, you still get to live it only once. Perhaps it's more instructive to say that you die once, and you get to live every single day. The choice of how to live is yours and yours alone.

Life can be brimming with excitement and accomplishment. Or not. You may pave a pathway of one success after another. Or not. You may enhance your treasured relationships. Or not. You may provide yourself with lasting peace of mind. Or not. The choice is always yours. Throughout your life, you will always have choices. Now is the time to use them wisely.

When you make a solemn commitment to improve, life doesn't get harder. It becomes more fun and consequently easier. When you stretch for the stars but just reach the moon, wonderful surprises happen. It's the stretching, the testing, and the experimentation with new ideas that is the elixir for your approaching greatness. A person with a novel idea is often considered eccentric (by others), until the idea is successful. Don't be deterred.

Many people have suggested that once the mind is stretched it never goes back to its original shape. This means growth is taking shape. Thought creation and thinking control have power. It is quite harmful to keep insisting that you just aren't good enough, smart enough, or important enough. For many, this becomes the end of their story, as they compare themselves to people they perceive as more talented. The lightbulb in their head turns off and stays dark. New and better thoughts never get illuminated.

Your story deserves a much better ending, and you can make it so. Nobel Prize winner Marie Curie said, "Nothing in life is to be feared; it is only to be understood." Without fear, you have it within you to springboard your life to new heights of achievement. What if you reconfigured your pessimism of expecting the worst by becoming committed to not let the "worst" become your story? With this simple change, your life could then expand to new possibilities. And you will be amazed at the results.

Confidence would then multiply, because you would have developed an exhaustive plan to ensure a different result. The doomsday result that was taking up unnecessary room in your mind would be demolished. The human mind and spirit, when challenged, requires that you have reasonable control over your actions and thoughts. It is the experiences and the adversities that provide the quintessential classroom where wisdom can flourish.

Action Steps

Make better choices from more options.
Create the story of my life.
Understand more and fear less.

CHAPTER 2

ESCAPING THE DANGER ZONE

*The Learning Mode Effect propels you
to a new frontier of triumphs.*

The longer you remain in your comfort zone, the stronger your routines and habits become. Thinking goes on autopilot, as the brain looks for familiar patterns to conserve effort. The lionization of that which is familiar will eventually cause your talents to atrophy and fade away because there is no need to be as sharp as possible. Your comfort zone becomes a danger zone.

Should you momentarily venture out of the comfort zone and face a situation that doesn't go well, it's easy to point a finger and blame someone else. Try pointing at something. Notice how when you point your index finger, three other fingers are pointing right back in your direction? These other three fingers are reminding you to take some responsibility for what just occurred. Also, remember that the Learning Mode Effect is a continuous "work in progress." While you will get better, you can always get better still.

In your comfort zone, you will never add additional arrows to your quiver. You will never feel the need to receive feedback, even though honest and sincere feedback is the breakfast of champions. It's like saying to yourself, "I'm so happy I remain totally unaware how others feel about me and I'm particularly proud of having no insight into how I am perceived by others."

Having unlimited capacity but never exploring your abilities is like buying an oil field and not drilling. The riches of life will pass you by.

The more diverse your experiences, the more opportunities you have for growth and career advancement in today's economy. You may also be thinking that new experiences bring the possibility for failure, as the thought of a negative outcome outweighs the prospect for a positive one. This kind of negative thinking is detrimental because it prevents any objective evaluation of improvement and review of your rate of development. It is not enough to say that you are growing; your rate of growth is a key metric that is often ignored.

Status quo thinking keeps you in your comfort zone and thinking small. *Very* small. Status quo is the inertia that keeps you stuck where you are. Your default option becomes the norm. Loss aversion is avoided. The familiar reigns supreme. You keep doing just what you are doing without considering other options.

Being safe means that you never have to test yourself, stretch your abilities, or think differently. When you purposefully prevent situations from occurring where you can err, the classroom of knowledge becomes locked. You are on the outside looking in. Learning won't happen.

Wherever you turn, peers, friends, and colleagues are advancing in their careers, and you are not. At your worst moments, when you are fed up with your progress, your mind tricks you into believing that the world is plotting against you. (It is not.)

Your comfort zone focus brings *easy* into the spotlight. Stay there too long, and *easy* will eventually cause you to be deathly afraid to do something different. You will avoid even the remote prospect of attempting an activity where there is a possibility that you might fail.

BE SELF-AWARE

Stand Out

It is important to become an "expert" in your field. Do whatever it takes. Attending industry conferences is money well spent. Volunteer for committees at associations. Meeting people is the best thing that you can do. If you say you don't have time, make the time.

The Error: You feel that you can't obtain knowledge and power.

The Fix: Being seen by others as having "credentials" makes you knowledgeable and powerful in the eyes of those who can give your career a boost.

Let's examine and change this type of thought. If we make "FAIL" into an acrostic, we can give it deeper and different meaning: **F**ailed **A**ttempts **I**gnite **L**earning. This could be your first step toward getting comfortable looking at the dreaded "F" word in a more sanguine way.

When you learn from the experience, nothing is lost. In the comfort zone, learning cannot be achieved because default behavior is merely your *go-to* pre-loaded behavior where nothing is examined. And sadly, you will never ask yourself this important two-part question, "Did I make a difference today, and can I do better tomorrow?" Not asking this question is detrimental to your progress and happiness.

You possess the sole power to choose from the many thoughts, actions, and attitudes at your disposal. Accordingly, being possessed of free will allows you to decide, come to a conclusion, or pick a belief, which can effectively make things better or make things worse in your personal life, family life, and business life. How you use your mind becomes a critical component to the kind of life you will have. It is time to reclaim control over your life and come to your own rescue. Let enjoying every moment that you have left become the focal point for a life well-lived.

You Have the Power to Create a Great Life

Often life's problems happen more because of the collapse of *mental will* than by the effect of any outside force. The script in your head follows you around everywhere. When you are able to control your mind, you have the ability to forge a veritable empire. Here's what I mean: The ability to improve relationships, solve problems, detect learning opportunities, and break free from your self-imposed mental prison will determine the life you will have. If the script content is positive, it will get you farther than your talents alone ever will. If, on the other hand, it is negative, which it is more likely to be, it is worthwhile to remember that no one can do something when they believe they can't.

Your calamitous negative thoughts and obstacles that keep you chained to underachievement is about to become a thing of the past.

Action Steps

Step out of my comfort zone.
Learn something new every day.
Adjust the script in my head.

CHAPTER 3

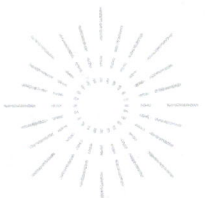

TRAVELING ALONG THE PATH OF LEAST RESISTANCE

Deeper thought prevents horrible things from happening.

Many folks unknowingly short circuit their critical *mental thinking process* by taking the path of least resistance. This path is never a good teacher, because new knowledge is not forthcoming. The path of least resistance becomes an alluring default position, because you feel like you are doing the right thing. But the easiest thing and the right thing aren't the same.

Choosing the path of least resistance rarely offers long-term benefits. You choose not to develop a skill because it doesn't come naturally. And then when you need that skill to solve a particular problem, you have no practice to draw upon. Knowledge and growth come from novel experiences, including the pain of failing (or not succeeding) while discovering alternative options and continually asking yourself what you've learned.

Eventually, the current activity of remaining on the path of least resistance morphs into a bad habit. The instant gratification that the path of least resistance offers outweighs the chronic harmful effects that choosing it will subsequently cause. The mind tricks you into believing that you made a right choice.

This false belief is what makes the insidious path of least resistance so tempting. By dodging the dreaded *fear* and *failure* bullets today, you set yourself up for preset behaviors that will lead to an undesirable result in the future. At some point, someone will call you on your poor performance. Accordingly, the path will prevent you from reaching your preferred destination (goal), such as obtaining a promotion or recognition. For example, if you are here (position *X* on your life's map) and you wish to get to there (position *Y* on your life's map), you most likely will never arrive because the path won't get you where you want to go. One day rolls into the next. And before you know it, many years have flown by, and countless opportunities have been lost. Sadly, perhaps when it's too late, you discover for yourself that too much time has passed you by.

Ask yourself: "How can I avoid the allure of the path of least resistance and grow and succeed so I can be, do, and have everything I desire in life?"

BE SELF-AWARE

Become an Author and a Public Speaker

When I first set out as a young attorney, the best advice I ever received was to: Always ask lots of how and why questions, become a public speaker, and write articles. This advice was invaluable. Asking questions of others, who know a lot more than you, accelerates your learning curve. Volunteering to write and speak in public becomes another difference maker. This effort will enhance your communication skills and allow others to view you as the expert. This is how your confidence and competence grows. Passion and talent, when combined with your actions and associations, are a powerful recipe for success.

Becoming better is hard work. Very hard work. But, as Mr.

Ziglar says, "Anything worth doing is worth doing poorly—until you learn how to do it well."

The Error: You become professionally invisible.

The Fix: Stand out as an expert. Write articles and speak in public.

The path of least resistance prevents you from seeking additional options. Assumptions block your sightline from seeing things in a different light. Rather, with a new approach, it's an easy, short mental hop to see obstacles lurking just ahead. You can break free from the magnetic pull of that path of least resistance when you gain the confidence to pose questions you never dared to consider.

- What does the situation now make possible?

- What can I learn today?

- How can I make this into my finest hour?

It is time that you gave that stubborn, cocky, and opinionated voice in your head more to think about. If life was a well-lit path, there would be no reason to summon up the courage to have a different conversation with yourself. But there is no well-lit path. The sooner the new conversation begins, the sooner you can reclaim your life.

Action Steps

Beware the path of least resistance.
When things are too easy, examine why.
Embrace challenges and keep asking questions.

CHAPTER 4

GREAT THINGS ALWAYS BEGIN ON THE INSIDE

Constant learning helps you honor yourself by becoming the very best you can be.

The mechanism for turning knowledge into wisdom is an evolving personal mental process. When employed, this mental laboratory works overtime to dissect, categorize, and assess every experience you have. It accumulates your preferred molecules of thoughts that float around the mind. These thoughts contribute to the formation of your beliefs, shape perceptions, and influence how you respond to those experiences. To squeeze the most out of life, you must couple those thoughts with appropriate actions. Because you can visit your past, present, and future in a nanosecond, you can use these visits to squeeze the most out of life.

From this day forward, you'll recognize that significant accomplishments begin within the mind. When an egg is broken by an outside force, life ceases. But when an egg is broken by an inside force, life begins. Great things begin on the inside. Your internal thoughts have the power to give birth to new ideas, and could mark the beginning of a fresh start in life.

BE SELF-AWARE

Think and Rethink

Anything ever accomplished began with a thought. Getting rid of all your "I win, you lose" thoughts is a great thing to do. Showing others how to perform better is a great thing to do. Living in a world of abundance where "I win, you win" is the preferred way is a great thing to do. Thinking about what you haven't noticed before (in the same or similar situation) is an eye-opening experience and a great thing to do. Pulling the curtain back on change is a great thing to do.

Whether your glass is half full or half empty depends on where it and you began. This means you may be in a better position if your glass is half empty but you are now going in the right direction. Things are looking up. Your situation is improving.

The opposite may be true when you consider your glass to be half full but you are now moving in the wrong direction. Your situation is deteriorating. This could mean that danger is around the corner.

The Error: You stop thinking and don't consider the direction you are going.

The Fix: It is so important to determine whether your direction is taking you closer to or further from your destination.

The Learning Mode Effect

Learning Mode promotes mental toughness and gives you confidence to tackle new tasks. You'll welcome "painfully" honest feedback and advice because you want a precise appraisal of your efforts and to understand how you are perceived by others.

Learning Mode practice also relieves the pressure of feeling that you always need to be right and/or perform flawlessly. You'll come to accept that every effort includes an initial period of struggle.

You will fall in love with the idea that each day is no longer just another day but a *personal training day.* A training day is important because whenever you try something new or different there is that initial resistance. In the past, that friction that you felt meant "failure" was close by. Therefore, giving up made sense. The status quo beckoned. Your training day overcomes that resistance because your new day was created just so you could improve and advance your life. And that is what each day is—a struggle to improve while overcoming the resistance that you can't instantly succeed. The Learning Mode Effect eliminates the anguish over your ability gaps. These gaps pinpoint the focus where practice is required.

Every situation in life, whether at home or at work, requires knowledge and expertise of some sort. Your job is to evaluate your competence against what is needed to complete the task at hand and eliminate any gap difference. Remember, your objective is to improve and get better. Then improve some more.
The Learning Mode Effect avoids this insidious trap: *If I'm a somebody when I triumph, then I'm a nobody when I flounder.* You will become far more effective when you make this statement: *By winning some of the time, I can win more of the time.*

Instant Benefits from Learning

The only person you compete against is yourself. When you understand this, your use of language will also change.

I can't...becomes I can.

I wish I had...becomes I'm glad I did.

If only I did this...becomes Next time I will.

And you'll ask that seldom-asked question: "Is this really the best I can do?"

When you assimilate needed information, you'll be able to plan for something challenging while it is easy. It is better to tackle a problem when it is marble-sized rather than let it grow into a baseball-sized issue. It is still much better to tackle a problem when it is baseball-sized, rather than basketball-sized. The sooner you start to tackle the problem, the more effective your solution will be. It has often been said that a problem is like an ice cream cone—you have to lick it or it turns into a mess.

Dealing with *change* and dealing with *problems* is the stuff of daily life. The one thing that usually prevents appropriate action is the unyielding desire to bathe in the warmth of the status quo. You become oblivious to the things that beg for attention. For example, you never consider changing the contribution allocations or beneficiaries on your retirement plan, and you let unwanted subscriptions renew.

I have criticized the status quo, often painting it in a very negative light. But, even with its major flaws, there exists a small fragment of redeeming features that can provide you and your team with the audacious boldness to achieve extraordinary tasks.

In the present day, countless entrepreneurs opt to maintain their current jobs or pursue further education while cautiously testing the waters of their new ideas and ventures. Astonishingly, these individuals form a distinguished roster of industry titans in business and entertainment. Think Apple co-founder Steve Wozniak, entrepreneur Sara Blakely, co-founders Larry Page and Sergey Brin, entertainer John Legend, Queen guitarist Brian May, and Nike founder Phil Knight, to mention just a few.

Even history itself bears witness to this uncommon pattern. It is said that John Adams clung to his law practice until the last possible moment before embarking on his journey as a delegate to the first Continental Congress. George Washington, too, managed his business ventures until Adams nominated him to lead the continental army.

However, beyond providing a sense of security to pursue daring ideas, the status quo is more likely to harm and hurt rather than help and assist you. As we have emphasized before, growth, progress, and enlightenment will seldom occur when you make the choice to remain stagnant in the familiar. Most of us have grown up being admonished against procrastination. Adam Grant, in his book *Originals: How Non-Conformists Move the World*, points out that in ancient Egypt there were two different verbs for *procrastination*. One use meant *laziness*. The other meant *waiting for the right time*. Leonardo da Vinci was a huge procrastinator. It took him sixteen years to complete the *Mona Lisa* and about fifteen years to finish *The Last Supper*. He was experimenting with optics. In the *Mona Lisa*, he observed how light hits an object, and in *The Last Supper* he continuously resketched the figures in various positions.

Procrastination can buy you time to engage in divergent thinking and time to work your thoughts through with others. Some ideas need time to mature. This is exactly what Martin Luther King did in his I Have a Dream speech. He let thoughts percolate through his mind for about a month before the speech. He started working in earnest on the speech only four days before giving it.

Da Vinci and King highlight the three ways that (*waiting for the right time*) procrastinating can be beneficial.

1. Delaying a task allows your mind to process other ideas and solutions. Additional time gives the mind time to connect disparate thoughts and make additional connections that generate new ideas.

2. By delaying the final decision-making process, you can avoid impulsive actions, gain greater insight working with others, and achieve a more advantageous result.

3. By delaying a resolution, you can recharge and refocus

with fresh perspectives that allow for more productivity and effectiveness.

On the other hand, procrastination, as we more generally understand the concept, is more often harmful because it comes with detrimental consequences. This, of course, is the laziness definition, which is the more common way we view this concept.

Putting things off until the last moment—not giving thought to what needs to be done—leads to rushed, subpar work on tasks, projects, or exams, causing untold stress and anxiety. The resulting low-quality work will affect your reputation and trustworthiness, which is hard to regain once lost.

Chronic procrastination is a habit that can be conquered with time management, goal setting, and planning and by addressing those thoughts that create the unwanted activity. Embracing working with others can ameliorate the situation.

If you're a pro at procrastinating (the lazy kind), keep the next thought in mind. The best time to plant a tree was twenty years ago; the second-best time is today. Remember your mantra is: *Next time I will. It is never too late. It's up to me to become great.*

Van Gogh once remarked, "I dream my painting, and then I paint my dreams."

It's time to paint your dreams!

Don't let procrastination get the better of you. You just learned how to use it to get better.

After every effort, ask yourself (gently): Is that the best I can do? *Evolving* happens to be one of life's greatest accomplishments. The Learning Mode Effect works best when:

You have a burning desire to be better.

You have a burning desire for a new beginning.

You have a burning desire for respect.

You have a burning desire to take control of your life.

Action Steps

Learn from each experience.
Welcome feedback.
Learn the difference between pacing yourself
and procrastinating.

CHAPTER 5

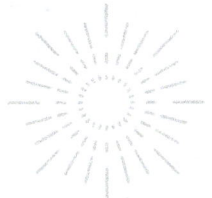

SPARKING EXPONENTIAL GROWTH
WITH INCREMENTAL IMPROVEMENT

The Learning Mode protocol will bring you an abundance
of respect at work and at home.

Since everything exists in potential, anything could be *possi*ble. It's your job to make what appears to be impossible and improbable happen. You don't just stumble upon the life you want. Living life is not a passive activity—anything but!—and it is important to remember to create the life you want to live. There is no magic bullet for a better life. It takes hard work... then more hard work after that. Success happens gradually...then, with enough hard work, it could feel like it happens suddenly.

The Navy SEALs live by a mantra: The only easy day was yesterday. Because the hard work is never over, it is necessary to give 100 percent effort every day.

This experiment will highlight why sustained persistence is critical to your success: I will entrust with you a magic penny that you can have for up to one month. This penny has a special property that will cause it to double in value each day. (In this section the focus will be on nominal value only.) For example, after five days it will be worth $.16. After ten days it will be worth $5.12.

Here's the deal: I offer you $1 million today in return for the magic penny. No questions asked. Accept the offer and you walk away with $1 million dollars. Will you give it back and take the $1 million? Your answer please.

Like our magic penny, compounding and sustained activity and growth yields small improvement at first. After five days, the penny is worth $.16 cents. After the first few days, your hypothetical progress at a new task is seemingly small too. After ten days, the value is $5.12. Still a nominal amount. Improvement may be slightly better.

After twenty days, the value becomes $5,243. Things are getting more meaningful and noticeable and so will your improvement. At twenty-five days, the penny's value grows to $167,777. Now, you start to see major, significant progress in the new activity.

By the thirty-first day, the value of our magic penny is $10,737,418. Impressive, right? Beyond-the-imagination impressive.

Let's revisit the question, "How good do you want to be?" Do you want to be $.16 good, or $5.12 good, or $10,737,418 good? The choice is yours. How good you want to be depends upon the effort you are willing to put in and the mistakes you are willing to learn from and the discomfort you are willing to tolerate.

Look, trying something new and different is likely to feel strange or even difficult. You will feel out of sorts. You will feel frustrated. You may see little or no improvement at all and wonder why you are attempting something new. But, when you are persistent, consistent, and expand your efforts, you will eventually see a glimmer of improvement. Keep at it, and keep taking steps forward toward your goal. One day, the difference will be stark.

BE SELF-AWARE

How to Get Ahead

Sometimes it is so important to get the attention of others.

This question presents a setting for you to achieve this. "What is it that appears not feasible to achieve yet—but if you could achieve it, would lead to greater profits and growth?"

Listen to the response, then ask: "What steps can I take to help you make this happen?"

This standout question will make you rise far above your peers. It begins with a thought and a step in the right direction. Typically, more thoughts and steps, over time, will be added. It takes courage to think that things can be different—and better!—and that you have the skills, mindset, and attitude to make that change. A new idea requires time to germinate. The idea will grow slowly at first as people become comfortable thinking and doing things differently. Then there will be a point where the idea develops lift-off on its own.

The Error: You remain in the shadows.

The Fix: You take the initiative to make your presence known.

Responsibility and Change

Want to be respected by your peers? Earn that respect. Stop overreacting to the slightest criticism and under correcting your attitude, thoughts, and activity. This is all within your power. Want to accomplish more? Improve your skills. It will happen over time. Want better relationships? Treat people as people instead of as objects and things.

It is also your job to take a degree of responsibility for every-thing that happens in your life, even if it's a tiny, tiny bit. A rain-drop takes no responsibility for a flood, yet each played a part. A snowflake takes no responsibility for a blizzard, yet each played a part. When something happens in your life, determine what part you played in the situation. As noted, you always played a part. And, when you realize this, you will grow.

Action Steps

Understand the power I possess.
Understand that everything exists in "potential."
Keep working on improvement.

CHAPTER 6

SAYING IT COULDN'T BE DONE

It is time to dream again.

In *See You at the Top*, Zig Ziglar wrote that "Man was designed for accomplishment, engineered for success, and endowed with the seeds of greatness." Notice some key words here: Designed (born) *for* accomplishment. Engineered *for* success. *With* seeds of greatness. Mr. Ziglar doesn't say that a person will accomplish things or will be successful or will be great automatically. To accomplish, succeed, and be great requires taking responsibility to make accomplishment, success, or greatness happen.

The Learning Mode mindset increases the chances that success, accomplishment, and greatness happen, because you were able to develop greater skills; able to think, rethink, and unthink so assumptions lose their allure and power; able to tackle challenges before they became unmanageable; and able to improve and begin better relationships.

While no one is born to be something (except perhaps royalty), anyone can become anything (else) they choose to be.

I want to drive this point home by way of introducing you to three athletes I admire.

BE SELF-AWARE

Make Relationships Count

Your peace of mind becomes vulnerable whenever you ask someone to intervene in your life. Trusting another is critical in such situations. Trust, however, should be earned. Constructing a sturdy bridge requires time, effort, and a sturdy foundation to ensure reliability. Once a bridge of trust is solidly built between people, it can bear the weight of challenges and deepen the necessary bonds required. It's a process. When mutual trust is established, each person is effectively holding up a sign that says thank you for making me feel important. Thank you for hearing me out. Thank you for caring about me. Thank you for permanently solving my problem, like you said you would. And thank you for doing it in a very timely manner.

Assuming trustworthiness in others when that trust has not been earned is a shortcut to disaster. Having a pleasant personality, coming from a good family, or even being in a position of authority doesn't make a person trustworthy. Before you let someone into your business or your life, get to know their character and their reputation.

The Error: You put your trust in the wrong person.

The Fix: Trust should be earned.

Muggsy Bogues

Tyrone "Muggsy" Bogues, at five feet, three inches, played in the NBA for fourteen years. Imagine for a moment that a very young (and short) Tyrone Bogues had confided in you about his NBA dream many years ago. Being a reasonable person, would you point out that short guys don't become NBA players?

Mr. Bogues is a marvel, a phenomenon, a rarity. He played the game he loved at the highest level, and he was also the shortest player to have ever played in the league. He evinces the principles of *Your Finest Hour*. It all starts with how one thinks and what one chooses to believe.

His mom and his sister instilled in him the unwavering belief that he could do anything he wanted. He understood he was in firm control over his life. He showed others what he was capable of both on and off the court. His mom was always there to mend the broken pieces of his heart when the kids bullied him for being too short and when he wasn't picked to play in local basketball games. She told him, "God doesn't make mistakes." She urged him, "Go out there and prove them wrong." And so, he did.

He worked hard at improving his core strength and his skills. He learned about the importance of discipline, dedication, and sacrifice. He could always be seen with a basketball in his hands, dribbling down hallways and staircases and passing the ball against a wall. He learned the importance of teamwork. It's not just about aggregate talent; it's also about making individuals better.

Many think the story of Muggsy Bogues is noteworthy because he played in the NBA. That achievement alone doesn't measure the greatness of the man. "I can and next time I will" thinking can take a person to the pantheon of great accomplishment.

In 1986, Bogues was one of fifty top collegiate players battling for twelve available spots on the U.S. National Basketball Team. Imagine all the height in that room, and Bogues made the team.

His alma mater, Wake Forest, retired his number (14), gave him the Arnold Palmer Award (the school's best athlete award), and inducted him in the school's hall of fame.

Before that, Bogues was the captain of his high school team, which for two years had a 60-0 record and was the most success-ful high school basketball team in the nation.

The desire to improve is the lynchpin of *Your Finest Hour*. The improvement of Bogues's stats between his freshman and senior year in college is rather significant. He averaged 1.7 assists per game and 1.2 points per game. That grew to 9.5 assists and 14.8 points per game. Improvement is hard work. It takes delib-erate practice.

Professionally, Bogues's team never won a championship and he was never voted onto an all-star team. Yet he garnered the respect of all the players around the league. Everyone who fol-lows the game, knows his name. It should be noted, besides hold-ing team records for assists, steals, minutes played, and starts, in the history of the NBA Bogues is ranked twelfth all-time in total assists. Although he's short, his life has always been about growth.

Bogues says that people often laughed at him when he first trotted onto the court, then cheered when they saw how he could play. (His retelling of these stories reminds me of the John Caples 1926 ad for the U.S. School of Music with the heading, "They laughed when I sat down at the piano—but when I started to play!") With a lot of practice, one can excel. Bogues's career demonstrates the power of believing in your-self. His determination and grit enabled him to have a career many considered impossible. His determination and grit also let him understand that one of the most important things a person can do is to invest in family. He leaned on them during difficult times and was fully present when love was needed. All along, he had a spectacular dream and he didn't let anyone smother that desire.

Here's a question for you. Have you let anyone smother your dreams? What comments have collapsed your mental will to suc-ceed? How many of your cherished dreams have you abandoned?

And a companion question. Have you snuffed out the dreams of others?

Your Finest Hour lets you dream again—and helps you encourage others to do the same.

Jim Abbott

Let me introduce you to another great athlete. Jim Abbott pitched for the Yankees, Angels, White Sox, and Brewers during his ten-year career. While playing with the New York Yankees, he pitched a no-hitter. A no-hitter happens when at least twenty-seven batters come up to bat and no batter gets a hit. On average, two no-hitters are thrown each year. Abbott was born without a right hand. After he threw the ball, he would then slip on a glove and catch the ball with his "throwing" hand. A person with one functional arm achieved something a small, small fraction of Major League baseball pitchers ever do. Amazing, right?

Learning new things was inculcated in Abbott from his earliest memory. His dad, a tremendous athlete, became aware of powerful words his own coaches used to shift attitudes: "Believe in yourself. Believe who you are. Believe who you can be and believe in becoming more." Yet, for Jim Abbott, these words were tempered by the things he couldn't do, the loneliness he felt, the constant staring, and the doubt that made its presence known. There were daily physical dilemmas, daily obstacles, and daily triumphs. In various ways, Abbott was exhorted to prove himself. Through it all, he learned that mental willpower gives the gift of *next time I will*, and *I can do it* beliefs.

When he was twelve, Abbott was written up in the local paper. He told the reporter of his wish to become a major leaguer. Think of how many people looked with derision at the article. Jim got the last laugh. His parents instilled in him grit, determination, and resilience to change a situation and not accept the mere opinions of others. His parents never said, "That's not a good idea" or tried to dissuade him. It was rather, "If that doesn't work, we'll do this." He didn't want to be known as "that kid" or to be just "pretty good" at a sport. He didn't want anyone feeling sorry for him or looking past him as if he wasn't there.

For sure, there were emotional ups and downs, pushing back against thoughts like, *How can I play ball like this? Meet a girl like this? Have a regular life like this?* With time, his inner fortitude grew. His dreams grew as well.

While it is extremely important to have loving and caring parents, it's also important to have teachers, coaches, and mentors lighting up the pathway to success. Abbott had plenty who encouraged and helped him become better along the way. For example, when a girl walked over to him to say she didn't like his hand, Mr. Clarkson, his third-grade teacher, told him to tell her that he didn't like her face. The lesson to be grasped was that she can't change her face any more than Jim could change his hand. And it was Mr. Clarkson who figured out the process for Jim to tie his shoes by himself. This required deliberate effort and highlighted the importance of having patience and determination.

The thing about determination is that it lets you delete the first two letters of "improbable" while making goals probable. Remaining in Learning Mode can take the mind to places it has never been to before. You can go to the future then back to the present in a nanosecond. However, his actual journey was filled with excruciating hard work. Abbott's parents had to let him fail and be there with a safety net when he fell. He learned his limitations and eventually eliminated them by developing his own techniques for whatever he wanted to do (including being a backup quarterback on his high school football team).

Years later, scouts showed no concern about drafting him in the first round. They didn't see his handicap because, as far as they were concerned, he didn't have one. He would practice catching and throwing the ball against the brick wall at the side of the house while imagining to be a Major League pitcher. Through countless versions and repetitions, he discovered how to catch and throw with the same hand. It became so natural, that it ultimately did not affect the delicate pitching sequence.

His first Major League scouting report stated: "Left-handed pitcher. 6-3, 180. Great arm. Good change up. Makings of a breaking ball. Natural cutter. Big competitor. Good athlete. Plays football. Good hitter." The final line said, "Has no right hand." It is one thing to want to do something. It is another thing entirely to figure out a way to do it.

People and coaches began to see a ballplayer, not a "one-handed" ballplayer. Abbott was the first baseball player to win the Sullivan Award, which goes to the outstanding amateur athlete in the nation. He represented the United States in the Pan American games and the Olympics.

His parents saw potential, not limitation. They saw opportunity and resilience, not limitation. They saw hope, not limitation. Jim eventually saw the same thing. Jim responded with the most insightful replies to letters he received from kids who had various disabilities. He wrote such things as, "Physical handicaps have little or no control over our mental abilities" and "You and I both know that handicaps are only setbacks in the eyes of others." Showing other children that they could prove their naysayers wrong, like he did, may be his most enduring legacy.

So let us pretend you had bumped into a very young Jim Abbott. "No way," you would say. "A person with one hand cannot play Major League baseball." Again, you would be mistaken. Let's again suppose for a moment that many years ago a young Jim Abbott, strapped into a prosthetic arm, confides in you about his audacious dream about playing in the Major Leagues. Looking at him, you would probably give him a million to one odds of ever playing professional baseball. As to the improbable thought of pitching a no-hitter, you would just laugh and shake your head, probably thinking that he was out of touch with reality.

But, when used correctly, the mind will take you to wonderful places. And when you arrive, you discover that it can take you to even more wonderful places. This is the power of learning to achieve your finest hour.

Have you ever faced a pending situation where the result hoped for was thought by many to be impossible to obtain? Believing in something with every fiber of your being is a defining moment. What people *believe to be true is more important than what is true*. Abbott's mental toughness was enhanced by the simple unambiguous thought that he could do this. He chose to succeed. He most likely internalized two of Zig Ziglar's leading principles for living life:

"You are what you are and where you are because of what has gone into your mind. You can change what you are and where you are by changing what goes into your mind."

Jim Abbott knew that "the price of success is much lower than the price of failure."

Tom Dempsey

Finally, I want to introduce you to Tom Dempsey. He has no toes on his kicking foot and no fingers on his right hand. But, for many years, he held the record in the National Football League for kicking the longest field goal. "No way," you might say. A kicker with half a foot and no fingers on his right hand?" Yes, and he beat the prior record by seven yards. On November 8, 1970, with time running out, he kicked a sixty-three yard field goal that no one thought he could make. Dempsey's story shows that we are free agents when it comes to believing. Initial negative beliefs don't have to be the end of your story. But once you have an unshakable belief in the *I can* and *Next time I will* thoughts, super results are bound to follow. You always have three choices: Feel sorry for yourself. Take out your frustrations on others. Or learn a lesson. Tom Dempsey kept learning lessons.

There was the time that Tom was building something with his dad. He was having a hard time and out of frustration said, "Dammit, I can't get this done." His father admonished him in the strongest tone, "Boy, you never say 'I, can't.' You may have to do something differently, but you can do it."

When developing your abilities, don't wish things were easier. You become better. You don't wish that you faced less problems. You obtain more skills. You don't wish for fewer challenges. You gain wisdom. This is how one plows through those obstacles of life. After all, if nothing changes nothing changes. Change is ubiquitous. It is all around us all the time. If you remain static, stuck in that status quo, you'll become like a ripe fruit that rots. It is so much better to be like that green fruit that keeps on growing (and changing). Embracing change is the smartest thing that you will ever do. There is an old saying: "When you are through changing you are through." The funny thing about this is that many people insist *that they hate change.* Yet, they continue to ignore the admonishment, "If you keep doing what you've been doing and expect a different result, well that's just crazy."

Each of these athletes knew they had to change and knew they had to constantly learn new things. Being willing to learn and to be taught opened up a new world of opportunity. Each also answered the identical question in the same way: How good do you want to become? The answer: So good that I can't help but be noticed.

BE SELF-AWARE

Outwit the 800-Pound Gorilla

Trying something relatively new again, especially when you initially fail to accomplish the task at hand, can be very scary. Any obstacle shall remain insurmountable when you focus on reruns of "I'm not good enough" or continuously view challenges as threats to be avoided. For many, it's like succumbing to the fear of the mystical 800-pound gorilla.

You can win the battle by outwitting the gorilla. When you attempt something new or different for the umpteenth time, it feels like the 800-pound gorilla daring you to even try.

No matter your situation or condition, you can succeed, like so many others have. It is time to use the secret weapon of desire. Desire is the difference between being a curious thinker, a meticulous planner who asks probative questions compared to one who barely goes through the motions, while haphazardly checking off the to-do list so you can get back to beating yourself up for having not succeeded.

The Error: You forgot how to lead yourself.

The Fix: You can climb the proverbial oak tree or sit on the acorn as it grows. *Your Finest Hour* is written for those who chose to climb it (figuratively) and do something about your situation.

Getting Better Makes You Feel Alive Again

These athletes went through life with belief systems that screamed that *what is possible is what I say is possible.* Each proved that a successful outcome occurs through an indomitable spirit and a mastering of one's circumstances. The secret as you look in the mirror is to distinguish between who you are inside from what you see in the mirror.

When you love the life that you live, life will love you right back. The process of loving life, *your* life, begins with controlling your thoughts. I remember a time long ago when people would say, "You could no more do that than put a man on the moon." Thanks to the events of July 20, 1969, when Neil Armstrong and Buzz Aldrin landed on the moon, no one says that anymore. What that tells me is that *anything* is possible.

Can airplanes seat hundreds of passengers at a time and maintain sustainable flight? Yes. Can a person run a mile in less than four minutes? Yes. Can you hold thousands of books or thousands of songs in the palm of your hand? With today's technology, yes. Can a car run without gas? Yes. There are an unlimited number of examples of the impossible and improbable happening every day.

Think of something—or some *things*—that you once thought was impossible or improbable but that you can now do or will soon be able to do because you believed in it and worked toward it.

Write your own impossible or improbably achievement here.

_____

_____

_____

If you couldn't think of anything to write, or still can't picture yourself succeeding, don't be discouraged. Keep reading.

Action Steps

Make my dreams come true.
Think "I can" and make it happen.
Do more to open a world of possibilities.

CHAPTER 7

TAKING CONTROL OVER YOUR LIFE

A life filled with hope never deflates
when it is a life pumped up by learning.

Ready for some more life-changing, mind-encouraging, and spirit-lifting ideas to equip you to persevere through the struggles of life?

Your Life Will Never Be the Same Again

Today is just one day of all the days that will ever be. What happens tomorrow will depend upon what you do and what you learn today. An *opportunity day* is another day you have to define yourself, another day you have to correct what needs to be fixed (because of something you did or said on a prior day).

Let's add some meat and metrics to this statement. If you live to eighty years of age, you will have had at least 29,000 (opportunity) days of life. If you are twenty years old, you will have over 21,000 (opportunity) days left to enhance your life. When you reach your fiftieth birthday, you still may have over 4,000 (opportunity) days left. (If you want, you can disregard your first eight years' worth of opportunity days because of mental maturity issues.)

You can also transmute an opportunity day into a do-over day. Remember when you were a kid, playing a game and you messed up? You wanted a do-over. Now you can make an ordinary day into one of your do-over days. When you take advantage of an opportunity/do-over day it's like living life for a second time, but this time you are smarter and wiser. There is nothing better than getting a crack at correcting what needs bettering and repairing.

The pressure is further taken off you because each day can also become a *training day* (see Chapter 4). Life is no longer the final game of a championship series, where you believe that you must get everything right and you "punish" yourself when you don't. You now have three different strategic and dynamic ways to view a typical twenty-four-hour day where you work on becoming better, improving your skills, and obtaining new needed skills. Enriching yourself affords you a phenomenal opportunity to satisfy your deep desires to become the person you truly want to be. Your opportunity/do-over/training days have created a safe environment, where for the first time, you can answer the question that has bedeviled you all your life: "What would I do if I wasn't afraid of failing?" Because, now you know, when you embrace getting better, there is no such thing as failure. There is no such thing as fear. There is only improvement.

There is the stretching of one's abilities. There is no pressure. Adversity becomes your friend. Just as a person needs medicine to get better, a person needs adversity and struggle to make better decisions. Seeing and knowing what needs to be corrected is powerful and liberating.

The depth of the struggle will determine the strength and extent of your growth. Before I embraced the task of building new skills, adversity would force me to give up. It was easy to revert into my victim-mode emotions. It was like putting my feet into wet cement and keeping them there until it dried. It is no fun having forward progress halted. Now you can make a setback work for you. That victim-mode scenario will never happen again in my life, and you can prevent it from happening in yours.

The Rockefeller Mindset

As the Civil War ended, conditions were ripe for economic growth of proportions never seen before. Although the oil industry held enormous promise, many saw uncertainty and sold their interest, as the wild petroleum market gyrations caused fear and confusion. Others like John D. Rockefeller, who have been lionized, praised, mocked, and reviled, had a vision that this new industry was about to start an economic revolution and evolution. They were the ones who took the risks and reaped the rewards.

Many successful businesspeople owe their success to the suffering, misfortune, and calamity they confronted along their road to success. John D. Rockefeller didn't want to be like his father, a snake oil salesman, a bigamist, and a fraud who ultimately left the family. He believed in long-term planning and chose to take a more righteous path.

As his personal classroom, he learned from the economic panic of 1857, the six-year recession of 1873, and the antitrust decision of the Supreme Court in 1911. He embraced many of the "inner world" principles and attitudes that will take you to your finest hour. Because he used its wisdom, he has left an indelible mark on the world.

According to his biographer Ron Chernow, Rockefeller's struggles mentioned here were transfigured into opportunities. The lessons learned enabled him to pulverize obstacles, which he thought of as petty distractions. For Rockefeller, every problem constituted a challenge, a test. He became well-educated in what to do and what not do. He used opportunity/do-over/training days to the fullest.

Rockefeller was a master at knowing the difference between what was in his control and what wasn't. His companies controlled pipelines, refineries, and production capacity. He also branched out into iron, copper steel, railroads, and newspapers. He was also a master relationship builder. He was able to soothe apprehensive creditors during uncertain and tumultuous times, notes Chernow. He was a skilled planner with top-notch business acumen. He showed what could happen when one chooses to continuously learn from the experiences they have.

Rockefeller also understood that there is strength in silence. He made it a practice to listen a lot more than he talked. He had taken the maxim to heart that "God gave people two ears and one mouth" for a reason. Success was a product of keeping the ears open and the mouth closed. It has been said that his long silences threw his adversaries off balance.

As Rockefeller matured as a businessman, he grew comfortable in his own skin. He never craved the approval of others and always paid attention to and acknowledged the "little guy," no matter their station in life. He was aware of what he *should* do, not just what he could do. He also knew that struggle became the crucible of character.

Sometimes results can even hold a huge surprise. The 1911 Supreme Court decision on the Sherman Antitrust Act grew Rockefeller's fortune more than threefold. When the trust was broken up, he owned 25 percent of each of the thirty-three subsidiary companies. His net worth grew from $300 million to just shy of $1 billion.

Although Rockefeller's classmates struggled to remember him, they did recall his slow, ponderous style of thinking, which he got from his mother. She trained her children to reflect coolly before deciding. Rockefeller himself was known to say, "We will let it simmer." Her prescience was enlightened as she grasped the fact that, between the happening of an event or the appearance of some catalyst, there is time to choose an appropriate response.

She understood that her son had the power to decide what he could become in a given moment.

Once Rockefeller surveyed the situation, he set appropriate goals and attacked them with discipline and precision. I like the story of how at sixteen he made a list of all the companies he wanted to work for. When he worked his way down the list without receiving an offer, he started at the beginning again. One of the most important days in Rockefeller's life was the day he landed his first job. September 26, 1855, became known as "Job Day." The anniversary of this day was celebrated more fervently than his birthday.

BE SELF-AWARE

Set Goals

Successful people consistently reach their goals because they work diligently to sharpen their skills and grow their talents as they strive to meet ever-evolving challenges. Follow these three steps:

1. Identify your most audacious aspirations. I say "audacious" because the fire of desire must be strong and powerful enough to withstand the negative forces of others arguing against the implementation of the goal. These naysayers, however, often lack necessary information, as well as an understanding of the situation.

2. Recognize the obstacles in your path and select a few trusted confidants to provide assistance. Concurrently, you must continue to acquire and improve upon skills (new and old) so your compelling ideas can lead to an effective plan.

3. Make a detailed plan with a defined timeframe.

The Error: Most people don't have a detailed plan for reaching their goals.

The Fix: Always have a plan that considers the obstacles

and adversities you will face. Your team members must possess the right complementary skillsets and be aware of others who can provide additional help. Improving is the only way to make opportunity/do-over/training days matter.

Rockefeller's initial goal was never to make a fortune; it was to help make the country great. He used his fortune for the good of his fellow man according to the dictates of his conscience. He gave away over half a billion dollars.

Most people make poor decisions when faced with intractable, complex, and significant issues. They panic and lose perspective, along with their nerve. Rockefeller remained unflappable as he worked hard at maintaining self-control. He reasoned, when you can control your emotions, you can control others, because those who lack self-control always slip up. And he gained unimagined wealth.

In life, it is important to understand that one always has options. The successful gambit requires that you choose a solid path, which you can do after examining the merits of each alternative. Notice I did not say choose the best path. In life there is no *best* anything. *Best* is very subjective. But it's part of our common language. For that reason, "best" does appear in this book. Just remember there are only *different* paths. These different paths may lead to the same destination. The difference may be in the timing, which could be impactful.

It is your turn to be like Rockefeller—and do what generations of great entrepreneurs have done. It is time to create your future.

Perspectives and Jumping to the Wrong Conclusions

For every living creature, except humans, things are what they are. Humans like to add a personal perspective. Therefore, nothing has meaning except the meaning that you give it. A story can become incendiary when a wrong perspective adds fuel to the fire. Your employer doesn't call you back. You think you're being fired. A friend cancels a date. You think she hates you. You get the picture. There is no award for jumping to wrong conclusions quickly. Neither does getting angry create more options. Anger just clouds the picture and distorts reality.

Earl Nightingale was a popular radio show host and prolific author in the field of human development, emotional intelligence, and self-help. To emphasize the point that each of us creates our own reality in our minds, here's the story he would tell: A Kansas farmer was asked by a passing stranger in a covered wagon, "What kind of people live around here?" The farmer replied with a question of his own. "Well, stranger, what kind of folks were there in the country you came from?" The stranger replied emphatically, "Well, there was mostly a low-down, lying, thieving, gossiping, backbiting lot of people." The farmer thought for a moment and said, "Well, stranger, I guess that's about the kind of folks you'll find around here."

As the first wagon moved on, another newcomer came upon the farmer and asked the same question: "What kind of people live around here?" The farmer again, answered with the same question about what kind of folks lived where the stranger came from. This stranger replied, "There was mostly a decent, hard-working, law-abiding, friendly lot of people." The farmer replied again, "Well, stranger, I guess that's about the kind of folks you'll find around here."

What our wise farmer said to the two strangers is this: Not only does a situation derive meaning from the meaning that you give it, but, just as importantly, what you believe to be true is more important than what is true.

Nature's Law Must Be Followed

Your Finest Hour follows Nature's Law. Planting a seed today will reap a harvest tomorrow. After putting in the hard work, it still takes a while to see the results. Lifting weights at the gym for a couple of days won't make a noticeable difference. Put in the effort for a month or more and you will start to see the payoff. Everything in life revolves around this compounding principle (see Chapter 5).

BE SELF-AWARE

Nature's Law

Super-quick and super-fast has become the accepted pace and rhythm of the day as folks expect immediate results in their personal and business lives. Products purchased online can be delivered the same day; thoughts and opinions can circumnavigate the globe in a blink of an eye.

On the other hand, Nature's Law is a direct result of cause and effect. It speaks not only to the agricultural cycle but also to our precious journey through life. The seeds planted *today* will reap the *harvest* of tomorrow (in a figurature sense). This law connects the future directly back to what is done in the present.

The seed of friendship planted today can blossom into that special harvest of love tomorrow. The seed of hard work sowed today can grow into the fruit of a career tomorrow. The seed of an idea embedded today can germinate into the roots of a solution tomorrow. There are no shortcuts or quick fixes to achieving life's goals. Expect a lot of thinking, a lot of effort, and a lot of hard work.

The Error: You crave meaningless and ineffective instant gratification.

The Fix: Nature's Law will yield long-term, lasting growth.

The Danger of Discarding Learning

One who embraces learning will have a better life than one who chooses to ignore it. When you are not learning, you will fail to consider points of view of others. You will label people and discard their ideas without considering their merits. When instant gratification is your signpost, you will endlessly criticize yourself whenever results take additional time to achieve.

Living a life through learning requires that you live in a world of abundance where ideas can join with other ideas. This kind of thought will allow you to freely acknowledge the other person's point of view, because *what* is right supersedes *who* is right. Showcasing your newfound insight will make people take notice. Your life will change.

However, if you choose to continue to live in a world of scarcity, nothing will change. In this world, your idea remains your idea. You do not share it. And here is the cruel point: If nothing changes…nothing changes.

Action Steps

*Use my opportunity/do-over/training days
to the fullest.
Correct my past mistakes.
Design my own future.*

CHAPTER 8

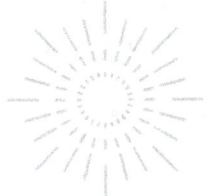

LIFE-CHANGING, THOUGHT-PROVOKING QUESTIONS

Unleashing the awesome insightfulness of the Your Finest Hour
Question Library will forever liberate your thinking.

Those who embrace learning know that asking questions rather than making pontificating statements is a key insight. A question that you ask brings you closer to additional wisdom. A question that is asked then answered will make you smarter faster. Asking a question shows that you are on a quest for something better and have a yearning for greater understanding.

Discovering new information can be life-altering. This is especially true when you can proactively use that knowledge to reshape your life. Below is a library of life-changing, penetrating and shrewd questions to bring wisdom to your doorsteps.

You just might be amazed at the results that you get. You could try them out for size, ignore some for the moment, and add your own as you see fit. But the great thing about the *Your Finest Hour* Question Library is that it can be accessed any time.

The mistake many make is to ask a version of the "why" question. Often, when this question is asked the subject feels like they are being interrogated. When the situation becomes adversarial, all is lost. Better than a "why" question is: "What were you hoping to accomplish here?" And as a follow-up: "What other actions could have been considered?"

When the "why" question is asked internally, it can throw your mental equilibrium off kilter. Often the question is heard as a statement. The voices in your head sound something like this: *Why do I have bad luck?* (Nothing ever goes right for me.) *Why did I screw up again?* (When it counts the most, I mess up the most.) What you are saying in assorted ways is that you are no good at life.

The "why" question can also be about the other person in a judgmental kind of way. For example, you may say to yourself: *Why did I get stuck with you again? Why is everyone around me so stupid?* The "why" question tends to weaken their resolve to fix the situation.

The "why me" question does not have a satisfactory answer. You can't do anything with it except beat yourself up. Many years ago, when I was in law school, I became very ill to the point that I was paralyzed and about to undergo brain surgery. The only question I knew how to ask was "why me?" But I couldn't do anything with this question. The more I asked it, the more anxiety it brought.

Just before my surgery, my mother-in-law admonished me with this phenomenal response: "If you never asked why me when things were going well in your life, you can't ask why me now." Looking back, her words were the best "medicine" I received that day.

The best thing you can do is to stop asking that debilitating "why me" query when something bad or unexpected happens and start asking a get-out-of-the-darkness question like "Why not me?" This new question permits you to focus on what is important. Getting better and doing better.

The questions contained in the *Your Finest Hour* Question Library below will help you to concentrate and adjust your thinking. They will sharpen your focus so you can get the information you need to improve your decision-making ability. It is also important to listen on different levels that include not only content but also emotional charge, choice of words, tone, and what has been left unsaid. Along your way, you will develop your own library of questions.

Here are some probing, introspective, and seldom-asked questions you may find helpful as you travel through life:

When you make a mistake or error:
What did I miss?
What can I do better next time?
What lessons can I learn from this?
What personal prisons have I built out of fear?
What does this now make possible?

When trying to solve a problem:
What don't I know?
Who could help me find the answer?
How do we know we are on track?
How will we address things once we are off track?
How can we make this work for each of us?

Before a phone call, personal conversation, or meeting:
What am I hoping to accomplish here?

Before you go to sleep/daydream:
If my life was a novel, how would it end? How might I make the ending better?

A reminder that you are better than you currently think you are:
Is that really the best I can do?
What one skill, if I could develop it today, would have the biggest

effect on my business, family, and personal life?
What is a unique skill or talent that I could develop even more?

Never forget that which is important to you:
What matters most to me?
What is the most loving thing that I can do for myself?
Who should be part of my life?
Who should remain part of my life?
What do I need to do to make my relationships better?
What steps can I take to make this happen?

Creating a not-to-do list:
Is there anything that I'm doing that is getting in the way of my success?
What am I doing that is no longer effective and should stop doing?

Looking-in-the-mirror thoughts:
What would constitute a perfect day?
What would I think if on my last day on earth the person I could have become meets the person I have become?
What is important here? (Before you say or do something you may regret.)
Whose life am I living?
What would I do if I weren't afraid?
Who can help me achieve this?

Improving relationships (business, personal, and family):
Am I adding to the panic or stress of this person or am I being a calming influence?
How can we work together to make this our finest hour?
What is the one thing I can do to make you more effective, productive, motivated, or engaged?
When was the last time I caught someone in the act of doing

something right and praised them for it?
What would you rather have: a one-time transaction or a relation-ship for a lifetime?
What can I do or say that would make you feel better?
Am I keeping in mind that not everyone has had the advantages that I have had? (When you are critical of someone.)
Is there anything you would like to add to the agenda?

Stop talking. Start listening. Get the information you want:
What else can I learn if I keep on listening?
What are you thinking but not saying?
What would you like to know first?

BE SELF-AWARE

Establish a Strong Relationship with Soft Questions

I have found that one of the best ways to connect emotion-ally is to ask questions. I believe "permission questions" are very effective.

Questions such as, "Would you mind if..." or "Would it be OK if...?" Although of the yes/no closed end variety, they are soft questions. If the answer is no, the prospect may be just a suspect. It could also be that you did a poor job in laying the groundwork for establishing a solid relationship.

Remember this foundational Ziglar point first introduced in Chapter 1: "People don't care how much you know until they know how much you care about them."

Too many professionals and salespeople do too much talking. Letting the other talk is what will get you more cus-tomers. Try asking "what if" questions. They will make your prospect and customer think about entering that relationship. *The Error:* You don't like to ask questions.

The Fix: Questions are your ticket to advancement.

Integrity inquiry:
How would the person I hope to be do the thing I'm about to do?
What do you think others who you admire would have done in a similar situation?

To get a better understanding of the person:
I don't suppose you can give me an example?
Can you tell me more?
Has anything happened in your life that I don't know about that I should know about?
What pressure are you under that I don't know about?
I know what I said to you. Do I really know what you heard?
What is the most important thing we should be talking about?
What has changed since the last time we spoke?
How else can I think about the situation? (This is a good way to attack assumptions and increase options.)

To get a better understanding of an unsuccessful event:
What was I trying to accomplish?
What happened instead?
Why did this happen?
What might I do differently next time?
What are the strongest parts of the plan?
What are the weakest parts of the plan?

Supporting an argument:
What is my/your best argument?
What is my/your best evidence for that argument?

Feedback:

What is the one thing I do as a [fill in] that bothers you the most?
When do you feel most respected by me?
When do you feel the most disrespected by me?
When do you feel most loved by me?

Responsibility:

How would you describe your contribution to the situation?

Outcome spotlight:

Once the project is completed, what would have to be true for the project to be deemed successful by all the stakeholders?
What must be true when this project is finished? (initial goals met)

Motivation probe:

How to prove them wrong, when told you are not capable?
What do you want to be true [fill in] years from now that is not true today?

At conclusion of a meeting:

What are the next important steps we must take before we meet again?

Mentoring/coaching/counseling:

What help do you think you need to solve this?
What do you see as your biggest challenge?
What are you struggling with now?

A viewpoint (business, family, and personal life):

When something happens to you, how does it define, diminish, or develop you?

Detective question:

Is there any reason someone would say that they saw you...? (When you don't trust an individual.)

Questions do more than bring you information you don't have. They can even make relationships closer and more satisfying.

Action Steps

Ask questions of others and of myself.
Talk less; listen more.
Never ask "why me" questions.

CHAPTER 9

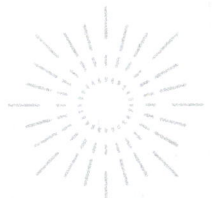

FIGHTING BETWEEN THE *WE* AND THE *ME*

Imagining your future starts with helping the other get what they need.

Learning Mode works extremely well when there is a shift in focus from "the me to the we." "Me" thinking can be stubborn to break through when one party continues to see themselves as better than others, or feels they deserve more than others, or just need to be seen as having all the "right" answers.

The existential problem manifests when a label is attached to other people and they are seen as less skilled, intelligent, or important. When people are labeled, they are not worthy of respect. You don't see those people for who they truly are. Accordingly, in your eyes, you are better than them or deserve more than them, and you get to justify your own bad behavior toward them.

When labeling is your method of choice, you no longer pay attention to the concern of others or even listen to them because you have transformed them into an object of scorn. If the opposite was true, you would have to listen to learn about that individual or listen to learn from that person or even listen to determine how you might even be mistaken in your thinking.

Labeling others puts the labeling individual in a superior position over the labeled individual. The labeling individual never has to go through the arduous task of testing their assumptions. It is just too easy to exaggerate differences. This is how more powerful people choose to give others little voice and, when convenient, make them into an opportune enemy.

Without a Desire to Learn, Conflicts Escalate Quickly
Everyone has a backstory. When you take away one's humanity, their backstory disappears. And when this happens, it is quite easy to justify your intolerable behavior. Imagine how bad things can get when all sides to a conflict are able to justify their atrocious deportment. A trying situation becomes that much more desperate when each person in the conflict is seen by the other as a troublemaker, as irresponsible, and as disrespectful, and each side is supremely confident that they are right.

When you are ensconced in learning, something that is important to the other side becomes important to you because it is important to the other side. There is a total shift in how the other person is viewed. They are no longer a thing, and they are no longer invisible. Henry David Thoreau said that the greatest compliment ever paid to him was when someone asked for his opinion, and they actually listened. Asking yourself about the kind of outcome you wish to have from your next conversation can immensely improve and positively contribute to the life of another.

BE SELF-AWARE

The View from the Other Side

Those who go the farthest understand the importance of taking the view from the perspective of the other person.

The most successful people in business and the happiest families see things from different perspectives.

Throughout the book, I alluded to the importance of having a mission and purpose centered around the universe of the other person. This is one of the great strategic moves you can make in your personal and business life. One of the greatest questions never asked is, "What and whose perspective am I missing?" When this question is asked, you can then focus on the needs, challenges, and objectives of the other.

Trouble brews when people with different perspectives are intentionally or negligently excluded from participating in the decision-making process. This applies in any situation. Bringing together an amalgam of stakeholders with different viewpoints is exceptionally valuable for gaining a deeper and more comprehensive understanding of the problem or issue. This collective approach will often uncover more meaningful and effective solutions.

The Error: Everything centers around "What is in it for me?"

The Fix: Think about how your family, friend, colleague, prospect, client, or customer gains first.

Next, learn how you can succeed by every measure by acquainting yourself with your thinking process.

Action Steps

Focus on we more than me.
Stop placing labels on others.
Make things that are important to others important to me.

CHAPTER 10

THINKING THE THOUGHTS
THAT COUNT

Thought creation and thinking control has saved many a person from making a foolish move.

There are two ways to go through life: You can bemoan the fact that other people will discover your secret that you really don't know what you are doing. Or you can go through life thinking that you don't know what you're doing yet but will soon figure it out. Just another choice that you make.

Be open to new ideas. Rather than wasting time seeking out only what "news" confirms your existing assumptions and conclusions, stay curious. Ask questions. Live life with a Learning Mode mindset (more about that in a minute!).

You can "win" more often by being more exceptional in your thinking and actions. A clearer picture of reality makes it easier to figure out how to make things better.

Life Under the Learning Mode Mindset

To become a champion in the game of life, you want to bounce back higher after confronting adversity. It's also about bending without breaking and becoming anti-fragile by having a stronger mindset. When each day is a training day, your focus is on spreading your wings wider and soaring higher. You will accomplish great things because you are no longer afraid. Life no longer becomes about sameness. It's about experimenting with different ways of doing as you build a future, one new thought at a time. Living life while embracing the Learning Mindset is the only way I know that you can remove the IM from the word *impossible.*

When you dare to think differently, you will come to believe that life is what happens *for* you instead of what happens *to* you. This means that no one owes you anything; that things could always be worse; and it's important to let go of what is not working and embrace something new. Your job is to respond to events and mold them to your liking.

When you live in the world of the customer, patient, client, or friend, you can accomplish so much more. When you can see life through their eyes and when you can understand their business from their perspective, they will listen to your advice and consider what you have to offer. However, things will be tedious and difficult when you refuse to see what they want you to see.

Many say that the best way to predict the future is to create it. The fastest way to accomplish this is to think and do as much as possible. Success happens when thinking attaches to the doing. The doing happens after the potential obstacles and downsides are considered and handled. Results could happen more quickly when you know who has solved the same or a similar problem. If you don't know, it is your job to find out who can become your guide. Attempting to solve a problem without prior experience typically adds cost and time, both of which could be quite detrimental.

A Parable

Once upon a time there was an ant and a grasshopper. The ant worked hard every day to put food away for the winter. The grasshopper, on the other hand, played every day and never thought about the future. Winter soon arrived. The ant thrived. The grasshopper starved.

This parable illustrates the power of proper thought and illustrates the supreme power of acquiring insight and knowledge. By now you are firmly aware that you lean on your past, live in the present, and plan for your future. Our ant, and those who perform the deep practice of Learning Mode, learn and understand the significance of prioritizing what we "must do," "need to do," and "want to do."

Where Bravery Resides

One of the most powerful questions you can ask yourself is: "How else can I think about this?" This query gets you thinking harder and deeper, which is what you want.

Remember the Biblical story of David and Goliath? No one wanted to take on Goliath in hand-to-hand combat. He was just too big. David asked himself that key silent question. "How else can I think about this?" Being brave is also about having the courage to think differently about the situation. David knew he couldn't fight Goliath up close. He also knew that being huge, while an advantage in hand-to-hand combat, may not be an advantage for Goliath when a sling shot made him an inviting target. David, because of how he thought, was able to cross the expansive gap between what was impossible to what became possible. You too, can do just as David did. You just need to think of other possibilities that can give you a new perspective on things.

BE SELF-AWARE

The Importance of Preparation

In business, financial rewards are not reaped by those who move the fastest (the hare) or by those who have the most power (Goliath) or by those who offer modest price points (Kia). The rewards will always go to those who are most prepared. That is why we celebrate effort.

The key is to champion intense uninterrupted focus. Your commitment to spending time alone with your thoughts will permit you to analyze them objectively in a calm environment and choose what to believe and what to discard.

However, busyness, for many, becomes a proxy for productivity. Opportunity costs calculations are usually forgotten along with what matters most to you, the company, and to the customers.

Success is always in the preparation. Life *is* going to happen. The question is: Are you prepared or unprepared?

The Error: Busyness becomes the proxy for efficiency and preparedness.

The Fix: Focused preparation will get you closer to your goals every time.

Shut Up and Listen

If you are doing the talking, you're not learning anything new. People love to talk about themselves, and you can use that to your advantage. When you let others talk, they feel valued, respected, and worthy. That is why it is important to ask questions rather than make pontificating statements.

Listening intently to others makes the speaker feel important and perhaps less lonely. Conversely, when you don't listen and ignore what is important to others, they will feel disrespected. This feeling will allow them to jump to a conclusion about your ability to be of service to them. You may not realize they have made a conclusion about you—until you fail to get the promotion, or they cancel an order, or they let the relationship fade out.

A Life That Matters

Focus on your life. Forget your fantasy depiction of someone else's life. Stop comparing yourself to others. The danger in comparing is that all you see is who you are not. This leaves you no better off. This is important to understand because your rating system is skewed to giving too many points to the other and not enough points to yourself.

I wonder, have you ever read about a woman who gave birth to a doctor or to a lawyer? Or to a success or to a failure? So far, I've only read about a mother giving birth to a boy or a girl. Accomplishments later in life are only by choice and volition.

I have met people who haven't succeeded in their business or in their personal or family life. I admit, it is pretty rare to meet someone who can't succeed. But I know people who *won't* ever succeed. It is important to remember that, like most things in life, success—however defined—is a choice.

I have come across people who no longer read. Is there really a difference between someone who can't read and someone who won't read? Remember, greatness is a choice.

If you never take that first step toward helping yourself, nothing will ever change. After all, there is little to learn by doing nothing. Success and greatness are a choice.

Success and greatness start with a healthy self-image. Here are three surefire ways to obtain a healthy self-image:

1. **Practice without pressure (mental rehearsal).** When you practice without pressure, you are providing yourself a safe space to mess up. It is better to do this as a practice, rather than when you need to show others your more polished side. Mental rehearsal is so important because it is a great time to be hard on yourself so you can perform your best when it counts.

2. **Acquire the characteristics of the people you choose**

to be around. Learn from those who have high moral character. Values count. Many people have gone farther than they believed they could because someone of character believed in them.

3. **Create your own victory or triumph list within your confidence letter (see Chapter 27).** It is so easy to forget successes that once gave you much pleasure. A victory or triumph list comes in very handy as a reminder of your "forgotten" elations. It is a crutch that keeps you upright when you stumble over who you are not. Life is about evolving into who you want to be. And, with all the advice in the next chapter, evolving becomes easier.

Action Steps

Write—or review—my victory list.
Question the relevance of my knowledge.
Stop comparing myself to others.

CHAPTER 11

FINDING A NEW PATH TO SUCCESS

Mistakes are better than gold. They make you richer faster.

The reason people avoid the discipline of Learning Mode is because it is painstakingly hard work. It turns the activity of making mistakes (which people seek to avoid) and learning from them into a new skillset. Seeking to educate and enrich yourself on a grand and profound scale is a challenge that tries patience. The discipline is like going uphill just as someone is trying to halt your progress by pulling you back. However, when you internalize the Learning Mode concepts and put them to work, you will start to think differently. You will see myriad benefits. There will come a time when trudging up "uphill" will feel like you're coasting "downhill."

Making an instant decision may be the antithesis of what you should be doing. Slowing down to consider additional options could be a very good strategy. Once the options are considered, you can harness the power of a simple question: "Now what?" Your goal is to unveil hidden potential in opportunities while they are viable. The possibilities unfolding before you will then dictate the speed of your decision making.

When the mind becomes more alert, you can ask another

question that takes you further along on your journey: "What would I do if I wasn't afraid?" This question can break the chains that have held you back. Imagine being introduced to daring choices that just a while ago you wouldn't have considered.

Appreciating You

Where you are in life is your starting point. You can go right or left, north or south, or even straight. You can stop for a while and then continue on your life's journey. And then you can stop again, if you wish. You can go fast or faster. Slow or slower. Velocity is determined by your interpretation of your current experience. You can even change your direction. Life, like travel, can take you to so many places if you know where you want to go.

BE SELF-AWARE

The Power of Purpose

There is the seemingly apocryphal story that contains pearls of wisdom about an individual asking three workers the same question at the same worksite. Watch how the answers differ.

"What are you doing?" the first is asked. The reply is, "I'm laying bricks."

The second worker replies, "I'm making $35.00 per hour."

The third worker replies, "I'm building a grand building, a cathedral."

Picture the joy in the face of the third worker, as he relates how he feels about what he is doing.

This disparity in mindset will lead to starkly different consequences.

Perhaps, it is time to make this day a masterpiece with your imprimatur stamped on the day. How many good ideas do you have that no one knows about? A thought without action keeps ideas hidden from view.

A thought or idea doesn't have to be perfectly formed, nor does it have to be big and audacious. It is enough that it could even be improved upon later.

Thinking of your purpose in life is to humankind what water is to a flower. It is that simple and that important.

The Error: You envision a life of sameness. There is little you can do.

The Fix: Your new, expanded mindset will shape your life.

The amazing thing about thought creation and thinking control is that you can travel quickly between the past and future. You can do the hard work to compare what was to what could be to what is and close the gap. Maximizing life's potential and purpose makes you a student of pattern discernment, so you can see the change coming your way.

Stop nitpicking the small stuff without looking at the larger picture of life. Your thoughts don't have to be astonishing or brilliant. It needs to be like breathing—that is, steady and regular. This regularity will cause the thoughts to go deeper at the right time.

There is the sometimes-competing desire to feel successful and important and to think of yourself as a good person. Lurking in the background of the mind is that constantly draining thought that you will remain insignificant in this life and die before your mark on this world is realized. Few of us will do something remarkable with our lives but the important thing that we can accomplish is to share our lives with other people.

Sometimes you will choose to do the thing that eats you up inside because you conveniently believe that the ends justify the means. For example, a decent man, when hungry and angry enough, might steal food or the money to buy it. He rationalizes this by saying, "Just this one time." A fledgling politician might misstate her opponent's record because she believes the opponent will not serve the community well. She rationalizes this by saying, "Just this one time." A lawyer may act unethically, "Just this one time" to ensure that his client comes out on top. There is no right way to do a wrong thing. And sometimes, even when you believe that the end justifies the means, your integrity might pull you back from the precipice of a bad decision, when the end becomes too harsh to fathom.

Too many parents try to reinforce in their children that they, the parents, are perfect. Imagine how better served the children would be when they see their parents as imperfect individuals, apologizing to others for the hurt they caused. Children can discover for themselves that there are important lessons to be learned from their own failures and errors and seek do better the next time.

Part of the price that we pay for our humanity are feelings of jealousy, betrayal, and dread. This is balanced with reveling in achievement, feeling loved, and having hope. The real question of life is not what you think of me, but rather what do I think of me? The pain that is felt by mistakes and underachievement can ultimately lead to growth.

Too many people believe that talented individuals are born with a special gift. This plays into the universal belief that great [fill-in-the-blank] are born, not made. This thinking is wrong. No one is born talented. But we can work hard and become what we aspire to be. Improvement happens from the pinpoint struggle. Scientific studies have shown that the focus on the struggle fires up and improves the efficiency of the neural networks in the brain. This super-firing occurs until the body adapts and the effort can happen with ease. The creation of new skills depends on the building and strengthening of those neural networks.

Mistakes pinpoint where the neural networks can improve. The more deliberate and deep the pinpoint practice becomes, the quicker the mistakes vanish and are replaced with the desired activity. The process of correcting errors improves the desired skillsets. To prevent those mistakes from becoming the norm, practice is required. A lot of practice.

For example, many famed musicians have similar thoughts that even missing one day of practice will cause them not be at the top of their game. It is significant enough when they just notice. If two or more days are missed, critics or even regular audience members may notice.

Repetition is a requirement for improvement in every field of endeavor. To emphasize this point from another perspective, note that Abraham Lincoln compared his mind to "a piece of steel, very hard to scratch anything on it and almost impossible after you get it there to rub it out."

You can also recognize this process in sports. Whenever one operates just beyond their ability and an error is made, the seeds of getting better lie within the mistake.

Sometimes, making a desired change can seem magical—like a magician pulling that rabbit out of the hat. You are amazed at your accomplishment. Except progress is not magic; it's hard work.

Practice makes you better in sport and smarter in life.

BE SELF-AWARE

Hard Work Brings Peace of Mind

As you come out of that icy turn, the car spins out of control. You frantically pump the brakes. The car continues its journey over the endless stretch of frozen water. You fail to regain control over the car, as it begins an uncontrollable slide over a steep embankment. And you wake up.

This horrible dream keeps reappearing, reminding you of the promises you had made to yourself, *that next year would be different. It would be a year of accomplishment. It would be a year of surfeit successes.* But you realize, wistfully, that you didn't learn all that much from the previous year.

Again, you failed to take control over your family life, your personal life, and your business life. It is indeed time to try something new.

The Learning Mode attitude is a powerful tool when you use it well. By becoming much more insightful, proficient, and enlightened in every aspect of your life, you create escape velocity from your past reminders of subpar performances. Better still, you'll never have to worry again about waking up in time to avert a nightmare.

The Error: Those bad dreams will persist when your performance remains ineffective. Doing the same thing over and over is manifested by your reminder nightmares.

The Fix: Improving will lead to a more peaceful existence.

Actually, a *lot* of practice is the answer. Once the practice develops and transmutes a movement or movements into a skill, you feel as if you always had that skill.

Let's forget sports for a moment. When you look at skillsets, you will see that people just like you are amassing talent because they have dedicated themselves to the hard work of getting better. There are no shortcuts. There is no way around Nature's Law.

Action Steps

Embrace improvement and stop being afraid.
Diversify my experiences and learn from my mistakes.
Repetition hastens learning.

CHAPTER 12

USING THE SPOTLIGHT EFFECTIVELY

With the North Star twinkling in the distance, when you focus on the right thing, you will be heading in the right direction.

Each day, as you play the game of life, your secret thoughts can become an open book and will no longer remain secret. Because your actions (including body language and facial and micro expressions) give your thoughts away, it is rather simple for everyone to discover who you really are. Accordingly, you have the power to attract others toward you or repel them. Humans, metaphorically, act a lot like magnets!

Whenever you meet another person, or see "others in action," a mental snapshot is taken. The issue with every snapshot, though, is the accuracy of the picture taken. It could be out of focus. If you are catching the person at a bad moment, you may not be seeing their true pictorial essence. They very well could be better than what your snapchat is showing you. Or not. You may also be catching them at their best moment, which may not describe who they are because those moments happen to be rare and few. Or not.

It seems to me that there are a few ways to dig deeper to find out who the person really is. Your job is to discover who this person is *most* of the time. You want a snapshot of their essence—their character. Your job, as a human essence detective, is to make people reveal their truer selves. You do this by providing some baseline activities that initially give them the benefit of the doubt that they are good, honest, caring people.

Here are the things you can easily do: Always place the spotlight on them. Say as little as possible while engaging them with deeper questions such as, "What are you thinking but not saying?" "What is the most important thing we should be talking about?" "Who should win here?" (The responses to each of the proffered questions could surprise and shock you and reveal more than you expected to hear, especially the last question.)

It seems to me that the answer to the first set of questions could accelerate the speed of learning. Excellent decision making shouldn't be far behind.

Next you can ask them about the challenges they face: "What obstacles are getting in the way of achieving your objectives, and what do you intend to do about it?"

You may wish to hear them opine about others.

You could ask the following questions regarding projects and employees: "How important is it to be the lone driving force within the company?" (Notice the word *lone*. Are they going to take all the credit?)

Then ask: "Is it true that others had ideas that delayed the implementation of the project?" (Notice the word *delayed*. Are they going to take any responsibility or pass the blame around?)

"Does anyone else deserve credit for the accomplishment?"

Watch how your snapchat comes into clearer focus with a gentle nudge of, "Tell me more."

You Are More Than Your Latest Achievement

The timing of completion of your goals in life may not happen according to your arbitrary schedule. Normally, things manifest themselves in their own time. But regardless of when it happens, there is one necessary ingredient that must always be present: appropriate preparation.

Achievement, no matter its size, is usually a remarkable event to be savored by all, except when the "achievement" is at *any cost* and tramples on others. Achievement at the expense of family cohesiveness is not a triumph that should be cherished. Allocating overwhelming effort to work stuff, while purposely ignoring family matters will get you "fired" at home.

The difference between successful and unsuccessful activity is quite stark. It has been depicted as the difference between living in heaven and hell. In heaven, as the story goes, people are healthy because they share their food with others. There is a wonderful understanding that everyone thrives by also taking care of others. There's an abundance mentality. In hell, people care only about feeding themselves at the expense of ignoring others. The scarcity mentality is a dangerous thinking pattern and a losing battle: *If you do well, I can't do well.* This is a sad fallacy that destroys relationships.

BE SELF-AWARE

Kindness and Caring Are Forces for Good

These are the talents, skills, and practices that enable the best leaders to lead.

You don't have to be a leader *because of authority*. You can simply be a leader *by example*.

You take the initiative to correct a problem because no one else has.

You tap into the "giving feeling" because it grounds you.

You see the good in others.

Kindness allows you to do your job effectively and to get things done.

Who put Dr. Martin Luther King Jr., Mahatma Gandhi, and

Nelson Mandela in charge of their respective movements in civil rights, nonviolence, and anti-apartheid? No one. They saw an opportunity for their people and for themselves.

The true measure of a person lies in how he treats someone who can do him no good. Such an individual will never calculate what others can do for him before acting. This individual simply looks for a way to be of service.

Leaders can reach the pinnacle of success without walking over others.

Authoritative leaders, on the other hand, sometimes look to advance themselves, and only themselves.

The Error: Thinking you need situational power and authority to lead.

The Fix: A leader leads because they see the opportunity others fail to see.

Blind Spotitis

A significant force could be blinding you—preventing you from seeing roadblocks and obstacles you're about to run into again. Blind spots lead to inadequate decision making. Friends and family get exasperated when you face the same mistakes and situations continuously. They see what you are unable to see. They don't know where or how to begin the conversation they desperately want to have with you.

In the meantime, these obstacles could act as a very tough adversarial opponent. The sooner you retool your thinking patterns, the better off you will be. When emotions run hot or uncertainty has the upper hand, just pause. This "time out" will allow you necessary time to redirect any "doing" and "speaking" to a later time when the emotional embers have cooled. Even a brief self-imposed "time out" offers precious time to consider your options—and their implications.

BE SELF-AWARE

Focus on Process

Imagine that you are a pinch hitter, coming to the plate. You are batting for the first time in your Major League career. You swing and miss again. "Strike three," yells the umpire.

This doesn't mean that you will strike out every time you come to the plate.

The next day, you come up to the plate for your second at bat. This time, you get a hit and win the game.

Note that your past—striking out—was relevant if you let it define your ability.

Yet, many people fail at something and then fear that they will continually strike out each time they come to the plate in the *game of life*. Let your past be your teacher, and try again with your spouse, your employer, your customer, your kids, or your friends.

Focusing on a process is key. It's the process that leads to the development of more skills and will eventually change the outcome.

The Error: When you mess up on your first try, you mistakenly believe that you will always fail.

The Fix: The process, how you do what you do, will determine how fast you improve.

Making choices, after considering the consequences, is the practical essence of adaptive learning. When you become aware that you are making intentional choices, you'll understand that things are no longer happening *to* you. They are, instead, now happening *for* you. When you become the cause instead of the effect (the victim), life feels so much better and brings more joy than you can imagine. Don't be a rudderless, powerless boat adrift at sea subject to the metaphorical currents of life that remain beyond your power.

With choices comes responsibility. Life asks you to have deeper conversations with yourself while asking penetrating questions about who you have allowed to be part of your circle of influence. These questions about relationships in your business and personal life require explicit answers. *Who should be part of my life? And who should remain part of my life? What do I need to do to make my relationships better? And what steps can I take to make this happen?*

Now that you are making explicit choices, it is critical to get to the literal root of the problem. After all, you just can't trim the weeds and congratulate yourself. You need to get to the root cause; in this case, you must pull up the weeds by their roots. Or they will pop right back up.

Here is a fundamental metaphorical question: Are you growing weeds, or a beautiful garden? The choice is yours.

Action Steps

Never let my actions repel another.
Don't jump to conclusions.
*See that life is happening **for** me, not **to** me.*

CHAPTER 13

FINDING YOUR NICHE

Self-education that leads to key insights lets you transform and optimize your business strategies.

Effort is never enough when it's the wrong kind of effort. Too much of the wrong kind of effort applied to an issue or problem could make you look like that well-known octopus on roller skates—a lot of unsynchronized movement taking you nowhere. But because you are doing something, you feel good about your "ineffective" and "wrong kind of effort."

The right effort combined with discipline, on the other hand, keeps you on the path to attainment because it leads to consistent execution. Disciplined *thinking* and *doing* is also significant, because it typically includes a well-regarded process that can be counted upon time and time again.

BE SELF-AWARE

A Champion Tomorrow

Possibilities begin with a thought. When that thought pushes to be expressed in the outer world, it requires an act and/or another thought to relate to. The most powerful thought is a thought that is either antecedent to or accompanies an act.

A thought by itself is meaningless. We are conditioned to thinking of things and patterns as pairs. Things that go together. They form an alliance. What would bacon be without eggs? Or coffee without cream?

In my world, an ACT is the acronym for **A** **C**hampion **T**omorrow. If you want to be a champion to yourself, to your family, to your colleagues, to your employer, and to your peers, you must commit to a specific activity. There is that thought, then there is the activity. Thought without action will do you little good.

Zig Ziglar said, "You were born to win, but to be the winner you were born to be you must plan to win and prepare to win. Then and only then can you legitimately expect to win."

The Error: Thinking without taking action does not improve your position.

The Fix: Become **A** **C**hampion **T**omorrow when you commit to act. Effective action takes you closer to your goals.

Don't Become a Commodity

Never let your target audience pigeonhole you into believing that you are no different than anyone else that does the kind of work that you do. You want to break into their thinking habit of believing that it doesn't matter whether they engage you or someone else. Because it really does matter!

People make it easier for themselves to select a purveyor, contractor, or professional by painting in broad strokes. That is why people like to think of you as a commodity. Too few companies excel at showing potential customers what makes them different. But you can—by having your differentiating business proposition. Take their commoditizing broad brush out of their hands and demonstrate that you are clearly not the same as your competitors.

For example, some companies compete primarily on price. Cutting prices falls in the realm of Einstein's idea of insanity when your competition can go as low as you. Only a few companies have survived and thrived using this strategy (e.g., Southwest, Walmart). The general rule is that if you live by low price you will die by low price.

Your differentiating factor changes the game as long as you can remain top of mind for your customers and clients. Better products or services don't win the day. Remember, differentiation takes place in the mind of the customers. You must show them how you are different and how the customers are better off for recognizing that fact.

There is a plethora of ways for customers and clients to remember that you are there to help. Because we live in a world of over-communication, you want your niche to be simple and easy to grasp quickly.

One powerful differentiator is being first—like Harvard, the first college in America, or Coca-Cola, "the real thing."

However, being first is obviously not an appropriate goal for everyone.

Based upon the above, one would be left with the impression that a first-mover advantage is a solid baked-in strategy. Let's see if this is so. The desire to be number one is ingrained in our culture. So, the question remains, how much risk does a first mover take on? As it turns out, the answer is a lot of risk. Because markets are usually unsettled for a first mover, they might scale up before the market can support that additional investment. The failure rate increases significantly for those who choose to go first.

Not being first means that you can understand the market better as you weigh the relative strengths and weaknesses and then move in with a better understanding and with a better product or service. The first mover often helps to create a new market. Later entrants can solidify the existence of that market with a more finely tuned service, product, or technology. Later entrants, however, run the risks of being mere copycats. Understanding the market is where all the planning effort needs to be focused. This is where there is no substitute for learning. It is so important to grasp the options available to you and determine which one works best for you.

Another differentiator would be to follow the examples of Apple, Google, and Amazon, who make it extremely easy to do business with them. Do you have a customer-friendly website? How quickly do you respond to customers' needs? Even better, can you anticipate their needs?

Another difference maker is having a reputation for holding to your core principle that your word is your bond. If you can always be counted on, that can be a major differentiator. The "my word is my bond" phraseology started back in the 1500s among traders. These words became like a verbal handshake with the meaning "you can count on me." The coat of arms of the London Stock Exchange bears the words *Dictum Meum Pactum*, or *My Word Is My Bond*. My word is my bond not only applies to business dealings but to personal interactions as well. Colleagues, peers, customers, and friends respect and trust those who keep their word that they will do what they say they will do.

Action Steps

Produce the right kind of effort.
Choose wisely. It makes a difference.
Make it easy to work with me.

Part 2

Fulfillment—Getting the Most Out of Practice

CHAPTER 14

COMING OUT OF YOUR COCOON

*You can reinvent yourself in the unlimited world
of Your Finest Hour.*

As people strive to become happier, they scramble to accumulate more things, including more money. But a happy life doesn't work this way. The first order of business is to create who you want to be. Keep improving to become that person. Then the trimmings and trappings of life will naturally follow.

Life isn't supposed to be easy. You'll experience obstacles, whether they are few or many. The number doesn't really matter, because a single well-placed and well-timed obstacle can stop you. Sometimes your path, filled with hardships, will take you over uncertain, difficult, and dangerous terrain. Your success will often depend upon your reasons to continue. Friedrich Nietzsche said it well: "He who has a why to live can bear almost any how." Viktor Frankl, psychologist and Holocaust survivor, espoused a similar but deeper concept about how people can give meaning to their lives even when just about all is lost, including freedom and health.

Transforming tragedy and predicament into triumph and achievement is a weighty task. But when you discover meaning in fulfilling life's potential, you are on your way toward mastering the art of living. Grit, resilience, and lessons learned become the stepping stones that transmute the inconceivable into the achievable.

So, it is up to you how far you will get. FEAR (**F**antasies **E**liminate **A**ccurate **R**ealities) of living life to the fullest encompasses many issues. These might include worrying about your age, bank account, education level, what other people think, and your willingness and ability to train and to forge ahead.

Whether you will be able to live your finest hour today or at some other time in the future is up to you. How you think remains important to retaining hope for that future. If you, for example, haven't arrived at that place in your journey, reframe that to include the word *yet*. You haven't arrived *yet*. This provides ubiquitous hope and harnesses opportunities for business and personal growth. In Chapter 10, you learned a different way that the use of "yet" provides hope.

What Should Be Important to You

No person on their deathbed has said, "I wish I had spent more time away from the family." Rather, they regret the feelings of kindness and caring that went undone and unsaid. They also regret the things they said that could not be taken back. This fundamental truth is the point that is too often forgotten: You and only you alone have sole custody over your life. You are definitely and effectively in charge of you. Every choice that you make has a corresponding result.

After becoming a student of motivation and skill development, you know there are only efforts to excel at. Your disciplined efforts will usually enable you to observe and examine your words before they leave your mouth. However, if those poorly chosen words should tumble out, let your self-talk remind you to sincerely apologize and that you are a work in progress and that you *will* do better next time.

The Shelter of the Comfort Zone

It is easy to hide from the awesome responsibility of living life. When things happen that cause a lot of aggravation and anxiety, your comfort zone protects you within the familiar.

In the "safety" of your comfort zone, you may not see new possibilities or potential that perpetual learning offers. You can't appreciate the dynamics of the *before*, and *after*, of certain behaviors. The *before* silo creates the problem that may reappear time and time again. The *after* silo makes room for you to use learning's incredible knowledge to your benefit. Mistakes are observed and corrected quickly. You evolve and become self-aware, as you continue to create a better future for yourself.

Attitude and the Cause-and-Effect Principle

When I was in school, there were no motivational or human development classes to attend. It was so easy to find terminal fault with oneself as self-loathing was easy to start but hard to stop.

The right attitude is key to living a great life because attitude determines the menu of possible responses. It's not what happens to you, it's all about how you respond to what just happened to you. It is so important that you distinguish between those things that are within your control and those things that are outside of your control. Too often people ignore that which they can control and seek to exert control over things they can't. You can't control how others will react and respond, but you can control your reactions and responses.

People Over Policy

Companies can become as unaware as people. Too many companies speak about "policy" provisions as if company guidelines and personnel rules were the holy grail. Concern for the customers and others take a back seat to the stated company policy. Often, "following policy" becomes a silly answer to why sensible requests cannot even be considered.

Company communication and rules can be difficult to understand, especially when explanations are couched in corporate policy gobbledygook that makes little sense to the affected customer or staff. The customer's point of view is effectively ignored, while the company policy is summarily upheld. The emphasis on policy erodes the trust required to sustain an ongoing business relationship. Only after the damage is done might the company realize that establishing and maintaining trust is more important than upholding a policy. In a culture where fewer people and companies are perceived as trustworthy, those that have earned trust are trusted even more.

When appropriate communication strategies are ignored, the customers also feel unimportant. This happens when calls are not quickly returned, when voicemail messages are uninspiring, when answers to inquiries take an inordinately long time, and when meetings are summarily canceled without adequate explanation. (And we haven't even mentioned the quality of the product or service provided!) Poor verbal communication and written correspondence is a prime reason why it is said that people hear from bad companies and hear about good companies.

BE SELF-AWARE

The Power of a Great Voicemail

Too many people leave boring, unenthusiastic voicemail messages with a leave-me-alone attitude. It goes something like this: "Hey, this is Dennis. I'm sitting at my desk. I heard the phone ring, and now I have to stop what I'm doing to speak with you."

Leave a fun, engaging, and compelling message when people call, so people will call you back. My colleague Jerry Allocca, an authority on modern marketing, tells everyone he is out saving the world, one URL at a time.

Now it's your turn to be creative and different. Try this: "Thanks for the call. You made my day. Leave me a concise message so I can return the favor."

I'm sure you can even do better than this. Got the picture. Go do it.

The Error: You leave unmemorable voicemails and have an undistinguished message when someone calls.

The Fix: Be creative, imaginative, and have fun.

Being Unaware

It is also important to be aware of cause and effect. It's never the weather, the kids, the time of day, the job, the illness, etc. It's you. When you deflect to make other people or other things the reason for your situation you are (purposely) unaware. Losing the ability to take corrective action will create harmful consequences that make your situation worse. The more unaware you remain, the less hope for the future you will have. That is when life can lose its meaning. However, even when hope and meaning are temporarily lost, you still have the ability to reshape your life by becoming the cause, once again.

In the modern world, we aren't limited by the place of our birth, or skin color, or age. We are limited by the size of our hope. A student who believes what he is told—that he is stupid—will study as little as possible, if at all. An unemployed worker will stop looking for a job when she can't find a suitable one quickly. A couple whose marriage is failing and has given up won't take meaningful action to make the marriage better; each party will continue to criticize the other, no matter what the other does.

Becoming aware of the cause-and-effect principle will refocus your attention to what is in your control. It's in the student's control to study. It's in the job seeker's control to stop looking for the perfect job and to find a job which she can make perfect. It's in the couple's control to complement and appreciate the other for even the little good and positive things.

There is a way to bring hope back into your life. Remember that failure is an event, not a person. It is so important to make friends with your past by learning from the mistakes that once occurred. And it is especially important to know that success will never make you, and failure will never break you.

Job Security versus Employment Security

While thinking about your tomorrow, consider this: Your employer or your best customer calls you into their office tomorrow and says, "Here is the opportunity you have been waiting for. It's yours."

How do you respond?

Would you say, "Thanks, but I'm not quite ready. I need to improve some specific skills and don't see myself doing that"?

I hope not.

If this is exactly what you have been preparing for, say that!

The learning attitude is the only thing that hastens that preparation. It makes you infinitely better. The talking heads on television may have you focusing on job security. More important than job security is employment security. While job security is really focused on your current company, employment security is focused on your abilities. It includes your skills, your reputation, and your network.

Here are three ways to enhance your employment security:

Be excited about showing up (or logging on) for work every day.

Give more than a full day's effort for a full day's pay.

Continue your education both on the job and off the job. Employers talk about their great employees. Become one of these people.

Certainly, your current employer and colleagues will admire

your effort and as a bonus you will develop a stellar reputation for character, integrity, and discipline. This attitude of doing and being "more" is a winning attitude that will get you to your life's destination sooner rather than later.

BE SELF-AWARE

Your Business Is Not Your Only Business

You work hard. But don't forget to whom you owe your utmost allegiance and responsibility. Your family is business number one. The business is family number two. Many have this backward. Who cares how successful you are or how successful you could become? It matters not, when you cannot hold your family together.

Do you go out of your way to do favors for colleagues, while forgetting about personal requests your spouse or kids make? Do you manage to show up for all your work meetings but not parent-teacher conferences? Do you always say yes to work and fit in family engagements only when you can?

There is a time for attending to business stuff and family stuff. That is the point. Each needs attending to. However, time doesn't stop because you kept the spotlight of life on you instead of moving it around to balance your business and family responsibilities. Love is the hardest work known to mankind. Unfortunately, too many see it as leisure "work."

The Error: You are married to your work.

The Fix: Live by a disciplined perspective and priority that puts family first.

Remember that your reputation follows you around like a shadow and will always arrive at a destination before you do.

And I bet you understand the importance of being a team player. Now I'm not talking about the team player who strives to get along. I'm talking about being the team player where **T**ogether **E**veryone **A**chieves **M**ore. Your starting point and ending point always involve character, integrity, and discipline. This applies to both your family team and your work team.

Surprises in life do happen. Your company may go bankrupt, downsize, or merge with a bigger company. I have also seen good people lose their job because it was given to a relative of the boss.

How can you ensure that you will stand out in the job marketplace when you are thrown into its mix and labeled unemployed? This is where your performance at work counts. This is where *what* you did and *how* you did it makes all the difference. This is where having balance between the aspects of your life is critical. This is when you must be able to have control over the mind.

Better Thoughts Plus Action

What you will do and how you do it cannot save you when a thought remains just a thought. The only way that *if it is to be it is up to me* has any meaning is to take full responsibility for your life now. Thoughts become the springboard for action to occur. You might discover a thought yelling, *I am better than this.* Now it's your job, through action, to prove it.

Life tells every man and woman to always be prepared because it is important to plan, and execute on those goals every day. Learning to use the tools to create your finest hour become devices that you control. There is a direct correlation between excellent performance today and rewards received tomorrow. Your family-work balance makes you better all around, because it makes you more contented.

It isn't only how much you know that counts, it's also who you are that counts. Become a learner. What could be better than that? Yes, you will still mess up. Now you get to clean up the mess before it causes lasting damage and hurt.

It has been said that men of wealth are envied and that men of power are admired. But those who pursue growth, enrichment, and mastery are both envied and admired.

Your conversation with others determines the depth of the resulting relationship. Proceed to the next chapter for more wisdom.

Action Steps

Take corrective action at the earliest moment.
Accept responsibility for results.
Enhance my reputation.

CHAPTER 15

SOFTER IS BETTER

Caring shows the other person how good life can be.

Imagine that you are in the car with your pre-teen on your way to a favorite store. Out of the blue, your child suggests a certain route.

How would you respond?

One parent might caustically remark, "Hey, who's driving here?"

Another might raise their voice and bark, "You have no clue what you're talking about."

A parent who teaches respect and courtesy in the family might say, "That works, too. But traffic is unpredictable at this hour, and I think going on this road will get us there faster. Thanks for the suggestion, though."

An important part of establishing and maintaining deep, lasting relationships is to model behavior that echoes the qualities you wish to receive back from the other. This parent, by his simple words of respect and tone established an atmosphere of trust, that it is *safe* to voice an opinion. This is so important to maintain at home and at work. Once trust is betrayed, communication becomes ineffective because listening is no longer important.

When it comes to parenting, I believe that imbuing children with curiosity and an *I can* attitude are among the most important things a parent can do for a child. This is accomplished when children are taught to love challenges and are praised for their efforts.

If the Mind Was More Like the Stomach

Our stomachs growl when they need nourishment, but our minds do not. Our minds get nourished when we remember to "feed" them *Your Finest Hour*–type thoughts. Let them go unfed for too long and the mind could cause you to erupt, like a volcano. When this type of over reaction prevails, the person has no second thoughts or urge to self-correct their damaging and hurtful ways; they are "right" and everyone else is "wrong." Those people are difficult! But let me suggest three strategies you may want to employ.

When the Mind Is Fed

1. **Look for the good in each person.** Dale Carnegie would often tell the story of how he made ordinary men extraordinarily wealthy. He said that when you search for gold you first have to move tons of dirt. When you go into the mine, you're not looking for dirt; you're looking for the gold. The lesson here is not to look at and focus on the flaws and foibles of others. The most important thing one can do is to look at their "gold"—their good qualities and attitudes.

2. **Be generous with praise.** Give people sincere praise where it is due. Many people go through life holding up an imaginary sign that says "Make Me Feel Important." Make the person you are with feel important.

3. **See the best in people.** Treat others as if they were what they *could* be so they can become what they

should be. This comes naturally when you do steps 1 and 2.

BE SELF-AWARE

Preventing Others from Making Mistakes

The Learning Mode attitude is a very handy and serious tool because it also looks at the life of the prospect and customer in a very protective way. When properly used, it can stop the other from making an error with serious consequences.

Leadership is also about being grateful for the possibility to serve another and to help others find equitable solutions for their problems and challenges. This applies even when the prospect has already informed you that she will not do business with you or your company. When this happens, many a salesperson would gather their things and leave in a huff. It is the smart salesperson that has the presence of mind to say, "If I saw that you were about to make a serious mistake that would cost you a lot of money, would you want me to have a further discussion with you, or would you prefer I just leave?" Now the possibility exists to start the conversation all over again.

How you treat and empower others will determine whether trust is flourishing or decreasing.

It is far better to help a customer, a prospect, or family member to stay out of trouble than to have to first get them out of trouble. You can step in and make a difference, if you don't lose your cool.

The Error: When your emotions heat up, you fail to see how you still might be of service.

The Fix: You make a continued effort to show that you care and how a better decision can save money and pain.

You are now ready to create lasting, deep thoughts that will take you to new heights of accomplishment.

Action Steps

Model the behavior I want my family, friends, and employees to follow.
Do not be an emotional volcano.
Make people feel valued.

CHAPTER 16

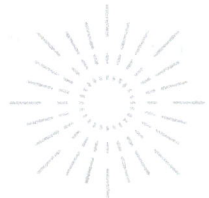

THE CASE FOR DELIBERATION

Positive thinking is a currency you can't afford to squander.

Positive thinking is a thought process based on an optimistic hope. It is not necessarily steeped in facts, data, or certainty. I can think all I want about being the best golfer, baseball player, or basketball player in the world. This, I must admit, is quite silly. Positive thinking alone will not let me do anything I want to do or be who I want to be. What positive thinking will do is make me work harder to improve and get better at what I want to excel at. It will open the door to hard work and deep practice. I could never be the Heavy Weight Champion of the World, but I could be a great author who brought joy and happiness to the lives of millions.

Positive thinking is far better than negative thinking will ever be. In years past, negative thinking would have prevented me from improving and getting better. It would have stopped me from writing this book. Being afraid of failing and afraid of what other people might say are two thoughts that would have kept my feet stuck in cement.

BE SELF-AWARE

Look Fear in the Eye

Now, you will know what I know: There are two things on the other side of fear. Success or something to learn. That's it! Rather than dwell on the things that hold you back, focus on what you want.

The blackboard (of life) is a great image to use for erasing those actions, moves, and gambits that did not work. Instead of beating yourself up, figure out how to improve and do it better next time. You can then focus upon your rate of improvement and arrive at the place where learning from mistakes, mess-ups, and miscalculations become the lift-off point for your journey.

Let's think about a hockey stick. A tremendous amount of work is required for that propulsion to occur. A hockey stick moment and exponential growth require a sustained input before a considerable output can be realized. Your Learning Mode attitude, with a lot of hard work, will give you hockey stick moments, where your thoughts and actions propel your rapid growth. This will happen when you look fear in the eye and stare it down. When it shrinks into itself and disappears, you can then use it for personal growth and gain.

The Error: Fear kills forward progress.

The Fix: Knowing what is on the other side of fear propels you forward.

How you think and what you think will have a direct influence on performance. An *I can* attitude coupled with your talent level could take you to the top. How high you go also depends upon your commitment, discipline, resilience, and grit. Positive thinking is a start, a door opener. Negative thinking just closes the door.

What Direction Are You Traveling?

A person who follows a desired direction, even when their direction temporarily changes, achieves more than one who wanders around going this way and that without a plan. The key is to propel yourself toward your goal (line) of life.

Steam cannot move anything until its potential power is confined. Likewise, a person cannot propel life forward until their potential is focused. A person's focus comes from how they see things. Many people are doubtful—*I'll believe it when I see it*—and their cautionary thinking stops them cold. They may be waiting forever, while their neighbor says, *I'll see it when I believe it*. Confidence, commitment, and creativity undoubtedly points their compass needle toward the land of possibilities.

Sadly, too many people have little or no idea what they can accomplish because they've been told for so long that they couldn't do this or achieve that. They were told that they weren't smart, creative, or whatever else they wanted to be. Consequently, they have no idea of the vast reservoirs of ability they have hidden within. They have talked themselves out of trying harder to be better.

It wasn't until fifth grade that I officially discarded the dunce cap that reminded me how dumb I supposedly was. Then one day, Mrs. Rapp, my fifth-grade teacher, paid me a compliment and told me she was proud of the work I was doing. There are some days one never forgets, and this is one of them. This was a great day for me. The mental bone-head cap was removed. Back then, the incremental betterment approach of learning saved me. At the time, I never knew such a forceful, life-changing concept existed.

Remember those sport heroes in Chapter 6? Each made it to the pinnacle of their sport by thinking and doing the important, critical points repeatedly. They knew that their burning desire made the thought that everything *exists in potential* so real for them.

Now make this thought so real for yourself.

┌─── **Action Steps** ───┐

Think positively.
Develop a "can do" framework.
See possibilities.

CHAPTER 17

I AM INNOCENT. YOU ARE GUILTY!

Your Finest Hour *can prevent the jumping to conclusion*
game from continuing.

The fundamental attribution error is used by many as an "innocuous" labeling tool that destroys the fabric of important relationships. You begin to see people as bad people because you quickly conclude that they have an intolerable character flaw. Yet, when you do the same or similar thing it is because of the situation you are confronted with.

Under this theory, the situational influences that caused your equally bad behavior are minimized. Yet, you use the facts of the situation to bolster the argument that you are a good person. Something occurred that *caused* you to do what you did. You just don't give the other person the same situational benefit.

The most ubiquitous example used to illustrate this point is the driver who suddenly cuts in front of you and speeds off, causing you to abruptly stop or turn. Other possibilities for this reckless act are never considered. Perhaps he had a medical emergency, or a family member is having one. Perhaps she is late for the most important meeting of her life. Maybe his child's play has already started, and he promised her he would be there.

It could be a hundred different things. But, in anger, you assume the person is purposely being reckless.

Situations always make us forget where we are and who we are for the moment.

BE SELF-AWARE

Look for the Good

Reflection permits you to think and rethink, to plan and re-plan. It also gives you time to ask, "What would I do differently given a similar circumstance?" Jumping to erroneous conclusions prevents important relationships that breathe air into you from taking shape. When you look for the good in others without vilifying the other, the relationship has a good chance to survive.

Success always circles back to how well you understand and communicate with people. And this depends upon how well you understand yourself—your desires, your motivations, your attitudes and whether your bundles of thoughts coupled with actions get you closer to what you want in life. Remember that life is said to act as an echo. What you give, you get back.

The Error: You cast aspersions on others without knowing all the facts.

The Fix: Become that space between stimulus and response and create an appropriate response with a question rather than a statement. An appropriate probing question might be, "Can you help me understand what just occurred?"

You Are Never That Bad Person

Have you ever noticed that when your colleague's volcanic

temper erupts, he is depicted as obnoxious or outrageous? Yet when you do the same thing, do you claim you were justified?

Have you ever noticed when your child is stubborn, she is considered headstrong? Yet when you act with the same tendencies, do you believe yourself to be very determined?

Have you ever noticed when an individual brutally comments about a minority employee, peer, or acquaintance he is considered prejudiced? Yet when you voice opposition to working or dealing with that same individual, do you insist you are impartial and using sound judgment?

Have you ever noticed when someone else's project is delayed it is because incompetence caused the pace of progress to be incredibly slow? Yet when your project isn't done on time, do you insist it's because the team was determined to get it right the first time?

Have you ever noticed that when someone highlights defects in your thinking you see them as overly critical and maybe out of touch? Yet when you are overly critical, do you conclude that you are rather discerning?

You will likely misjudge an individual when you jump to the conclusion that he has a character flaw. The questioned behavior was manifested because of situational facts. When you let *Your Finest Hour* principles be your guide, you will ask yourself, "How else can I view this individual?" You will also consider your responses and actions differently.

Action Steps

Reflect and rethink more.
Stop assuming anyone is a "bad" person.
Be aware that situations can cause good people to make bad choices.

CHAPTER 18

HOCUS FOCUS

Ignite your mind to the possibilities of life.

When I wrote *Don't Play with Fire,* I saw the benefit of pro-tracted time ensconced in my home office. I tried to hide from competing distractions of immediately responding to texts and emails. I have learned that much of what is generally noted as "important" and "urgent" isn't all that important or urgent. Writing *Your Finest Hour* became easier to complete because I learned how to remain distraction-free.

Once I started to think and write, those texts and emails pounding on my mental door for attention were forgotten and ignored. I write best when I am in marathon mode. That is how I seep into the flow state zone, as ideas come gushing forth on the page. I love losing myself in my writing. Who I am, what I think, and how I think depends upon what I focus on. And what I focus on is dependent upon the task at hand.

Throughout my career, especially my legal career, I have found that focus allowed me to master difficult concepts and finish tasks at a speed pleasing to my clients. I learned that busy-ness gave me the feeling of being prolific. Often, it provided a false sense of security that the day was productive when it was anything but constructive and effective. Social media companies thrive on this busyness, visible effort/open office concept.

I suppose that getting back to clients and customers supersonically fast may make them feel important. But, having something important to tell them is even more important.

Mistakes Can Become Gold

A German proverb reminds us that we become clever through mistakes. The learning attitude increases wisdom attainment and learning velocity by transforming mistakes into behavioral assets. You will improve faster and reach your goals more quickly when you work just outside your abilities by trying something new. As you work harder, and get better, those mistakes (many people call them failures, which they are not) transmute into skills.

Science is showing us that struggle is not a preference or a choice. It is a biological requirement, as the brain creates new neural networks for electrical impulses to fire. These circuits are what improve thought, performance, and skillsets.

If you are like most people, you probably give up when you can't do an activity well the first time. I used to do this all the time. Had I understood that the body needs time to develop new circuitry, perhaps I would have persevered instead.

You may feel awkward and embarrassed when you can't get that task right the first time. Your heart might race. But here is the thing. You are the only one who knows it.

Scientists have attempted to answer how some people become so talented and how they obtain greatness. After decades of study, it is now a central tenet that greatness in any field requires about 10,000 hours of focused, deliberate practice. Think golfer Tiger Woods, tennis player Anna Kournikova, film producer Ron Howard, violinist Itzhak Perlman, racecar driver Lewis Hamilton, novelist Dan Brown, pop star Usher, biographer Doris Kearns Goodwin, or motivation author Daniel H. Pink, to name a few. As Daniel Coyle states in detail in the *Talent*

Code, uber-successful people have a vision of their future selves and, through the concept of ignition, there is an awakening in the subconscious that asks, *If she can do it, why can't I?*

Think in Chunk-Size Pieces

Start by thinking in chunks. Look at the task as one complete thing. Then divide it into smaller pieces. It's like zooming out and zooming in.

Whether it's a new act required of you, or a novel situation you're facing, start the same way.

If you don't have 10,000 hours to practice for greatness and stardom, you can still improve immensely. Let's say you have been asked to give a company speech. You have never done this before. The first order of business is to filter out those immediate negative thoughts: *I can't do this. I've never done this. What if my boss laughs. My buddies know I can't pull this off.* If you are in panic mode, you won't be able to do it and you would have created a self-fulfilling prophecy. *No one can when they believe that they can't.* Look at the skills that may be required. If you don't possess them, acquire them.

BE SELF-AWARE

Make Life Your Story

As the authoritative writer and author of your life, you can edit and reshape the script in your head according to your desires. The story being lived is not just a story but *your* story.

You are the writer of the script, as well as the casting director. You decide which roles to play and how to portray each role.

You alone have the power to write the script about your life. Do it. You have the power to direct your movie. Take control. You have the power to attempt new and different things and try out new ideas. Go ahead. You have the power to become the best you possible. That part is always a work in progress. Your "victim" character, when you think about it, is doomed from the start because the role requires you to be adversely affected by the acts of others, just how the currents affect a boat adrift at sea. At some point in life you will scream, "Enough!" and take over the controls.

The Error: You let outside forces remain in control.

The Fix: You take absolute control over your life.

Now start thinking in chunks. First, look at what you were asked to do: Give a speech, no longer than twenty minutes. The subject: Production capacity for the new project. You are the expert. Break the speech down into its main component parts: the key things that must be done before, during, and after production that will enhance quality control.

Compose the speech in long hand. Write every thought that comes into your head. You will edit it later. When you are done, make an outline using key words or thoughts only as a guide. You want to talk *to* the group, not *at* the group. When you are done with the draft phase and the outline phase, put it away for a day or two. Then reread it and ask these five questions: 1. How else can I think about what I want to say? 2. What information is still missing? 3. Have I distinguished facts and data from assumptions? 4. What questions will likely be asked of me? 5. How will I respond if I do not know the answer to a question?

When you practice, speak in conversational tones. Practice a lot. Practice at different paces. Then practice more. Give the speech from the outline you prepared. Do not read the speech.

You can look at this presentation as just a speech or as an audition in front of decision makers for a better opportunity.

Last quarter your colleague Doug spoke before the same group and did a phenomenal job. Now it is your turn to ignite your mind. Think: *If he can do it, I certainly can do it too.* And you will.

Recently, a client (a licensed professional) was facing the prospect of losing the biggest account he ever had. He was totally freaked out. He told me it was causing him anxiety and he was having trouble sleeping. Every second of every day he was consumed by something he never experienced before. He was constantly thinking the worst—how much it was going to *cost* him if things didn't go right. Facing a "bad" novel experience in life could be daunting. The self-talk questions and statements can come fast and furious: *What happens now? Why me? Why didn't I do things differently? What signals did I miss? Everyone will see that I have no idea what I'm doing. They'll see I'm just an impostor.*

And on and on it goes.

If it's a situation, chunk it by looking at best case/worst case scenarios. Factor in the options the other side has and your counter response to each. Review your gambits and possible responses the other side may employ. Review the outcome the other side prefers. Review the outcome you prefer. Build a bridge to get the best possible result. Start creating a plan. Look at the obstacles, challenges, and concern you'll encounter. Ask for help from those who can assist you. Make sure you are sensitive to the deadlines imposed. Ask lots of questions. You may want to review the life-changing, thought-provoking *Your Finest Hour* Question Library in Chapter 8.

Enriching yourself changes the way you see yourself. It gives you tools to face adversity and to get the most out of life by giving you agency. It focuses on helping you recover from errors, mistakes, and uncertainty quickly and graciously. It is not about avoiding errors. It is about learning from them and improving. It's about acknowledging feedback. It could be the difference between having a good life and a hard life.

So, should you mess up your presentation in any one of incalculable ways, or should my client fail to keep his biggest client ever, the Learning Mode attitude will make it very difficult for history to repeat itself.

Then, remember this: Most of what you deeply worry about will not happen. Studies call this premature worry. Humans have a habit of making predictions that turn out to be wrong.

The driving force of *Your Finest Hour* is about living life to the fullest. It's about using those opportunity/training/do-over days to the fullest. You know you are on your way when you realize that you are both the student and the teacher. The next chapter shows you what can happen when you wear both hats.

Action Steps

Prioritize my focus.
Be productive in ways that increase productivity.
Make a detailed plan.

CHAPTER 19

TEAMWORK INSPIRES

*Making the most out of every opportunity is the hallmark
of your finest hour.*

Many people who argue are really trying to explain why they are right. They have no desire to listen to counterarguments. This is very problematic and is the reason that differences in the home and at work cause unnecessary strife.

There are basically two paths to take when you are trying to persuade the other. There is the Commander Spock–Vulcan approach and the Captain Kirk–human approach. On *Star Trek,* Spock was the excessively logical and rational one. Kirk was infinitely more excitable.

Neuroscientist Antonio Damasio puts it this way: "Humans are not either thinking machines or feeling machines but rather feeling machines that think." He is suggesting that you must reach the heart as well as the head. Facts and data alone don't have the power to persuade without an emotional appeal added to the mix.

Statistics alone can't do this job. Facts and figures are often cherry-picked anyway. As used, they can be full of distortions, misrepresentations, and misinterpretations. Accordingly, they can distract from the salient points that need to be made.

Show emotions such as regret, sorrow, anger, or disgust in an appropriate way. Emotions can highlight the importance of your facts and figures. As Aristotle pointed out, the best way to be convincing is by combining logic (logos) and emotions (pathos) with your good character (ethos). A balanced approach in your thinking and a balanced approach in working with others will make you more persuasive and effective. When emotions are expressed in a healthy way, facts and statistics hold more gravitas and the point made becomes easier to understand.

Instead of asking "How can I accomplish this?" (which bypasses collaboration), consider asking, "Who can help me achieve this?" (Back to *Star Trek:* It was never Spock or Kirk but rather Spock *and* Kirk working together that made the difference.) This simple shift will open new possibilities and boost your confidence by working with people who care as you do and may have more experience than you. When you don't care who gets the credit, your goals can flourish. Your partnerships can transmute into powerful alliances where everyone contributes more than they receive.

The problem with tucked away and concealed emotions is that they can gush forth at the most inopportune time. Everything in their path, including your supporting evidence and proofs, can be lost on the audience.

BE SELF-AWARE

All Teams Are Not Equal

Teams may be interdependent or independent. Both types are needed. It is your job to determine what the task at hand requires. Some roles may be interchangeable, and some require specific expertise and specialization. Regardless of the type of team, they must collectively have the right amount of logic and emotion so each can successfully complete their tasks.

An interdependent group of people brings to mind a basketball team. Each member of the team needs to shoot, rebound, and pass. They each have the same basic skills, although one may be more proficient than others in a particular skill. This is where one teammate can help the other become better at a particular skill. Yet, they need to be aware of the needs of their individual teammates as they travel up and down the court.

An independent group resembles a track and field team. It may have a shot putter, high jumper, relay runner, etc. Each have different skills and perspectives. One member can't do the work of the other. It is important that members of the team show mutual support for the success of the other.

Every team brings to bear its own sphere of influence where resourcefulness, creativity, and cooperation affect production capacity. When logos, pathos, and ethos are aligned, doing the right thing and doing things right complement and balance each other.

The Error: You are not careful or discerning about the composition of your team.

The Fix: Be particularly aware of the physical and mental talents of each member of the team.

When hot emotions get the upper hand, your mind is the only tool you can use to keep your body temperature in the *cool keep thinking* range. Thought creation and thinking contol can keep emotions in check. Cool emotions at the time of deep stress and concern can enhance the ability to think deeply so you can make the points that need to be made.

Continuous assessment of risks and vulnerabilities is essential as they can impact the path that you choose. When a risk presents itself as a challenge or an obstacle, you and your team must be able to respond with effective mitigation and heightened vigilance. Deep collaboration plays a vital role in ensuring a project's adaptability and timely execution. Whenever there is collaboration, being the student and the teacher becomes critically important. That's precisely why the collective power of *who* (referring to individuals working together) surpasses the individual effort of *me*. Here, again, it is important to let logos and pathos work together to give you the freedom to seek the wisdom of others far more capable.

When you start with the weakened plea of "How can I accomplish this?", your limiting query could drag progress to a crawl, chaining you to possible mediocrity and ridicule. But when you confidently request, "Who can help me achieve this?" the wheels of forward movement and progress gain momentum because "potential" permeates every aspect of your personal, business, and family life where strong solid relationships exist. This is where character (ethos) becomes important.

BE SELF-AWARE

Working with Others Is Very Important

When each person sees themselves as an important member of the team, there is nothing that can't be accomplished.

Every team member must follow the core principles that make up living in a world together. Team members must: 1. support each other, 2. learn from each other, 3. and be accountable to each other. This happens every time logic, emotions, and character are balanced within the team.

Imagine what could be done when you commit to a world of values composed of should do's. A value/should do world inspires you *to do more and then some.* This is an unwavering standard that is built upon trust, reputation, and integrity, where listening to understand is the key ingredient. Listening to respond becomes a relic of the past.

The Error: You continue to believe that your ideas alone can solve the problem at hand.

The Fix: Values coalesce around a team that supports, encourages, and accounts to each other.

This fable sums up this chapter nicely and tells the story of an emperor who is looking for wisdom. He wants to ensure that neighbors in the kingdom live in harmony. Accordingly, he needs the answers to three pressing questions:

1. What is the best time to do each thing?

2. Who are the most important people to work with?

3. What is the most important thing to always do?

The emperor promised riches to anyone in the kingdom who could answer these questions correctly. As the answers poured in, the emperor was unenthused with the results. Out of desperation, he posed these same questions to an enlightened soul who lived far away, high in the mountains. Months later, the king received his response. When the emperor read those answers, he found exactly what he was looking for.

The answers:

1. There is only one important time, and that is now.

2. The most important person is the person beside you.

3. The most important pursuit is to make the person

standing at your side happy, for that alone is the pursuit of life.

Today humankind is concerned about service to others on a national and international scale. This notion is so vast that we often forget to serve those that are closer to us—family and friends and community. The people who matter most to us are always right in front of us.

Action Steps

Balance arguments with logic and emotions so you can work in harmony with others.
Ask "Who can help?" (rather than "How can I do all this?").
Discover how I can be of service to others.

CHAPTER 20

WIN BY LOSING OR LOSE BY WINNING

*Your finest hour is always about finding
another and better way.*

After a loss or when something bad happens, you never want to make the same mistakes over again. Learning from the experience becomes crucial, even though the lesson—or lessons—may be harsh.

What is to be done after a loss? Use a Post-Mortem analysis, which thoroughly examines any mistakes and errors. This permits an understanding of what went wrong and ways to avoid a similar result in the future. Concurrently, an After-Action Review can be prepared which also focuses on what went right. This forces you to concentrate on which processes need to be successfully duplicated.

In various activities of life, such as sports, politics, or business, unexpected failures can occur. For example, in sports, players can mismanage their strategies and lose a tournament or game. In politics, officeholders can miscalculate their approach and lose their election. And in business, owners can misjudge revenues and expenses and fight for survival.

On the surface, immediate success in life may seem like a

dream come true. However, there lies a hidden truth few dare to speak about or acknowledge: Early successes can lay the groundwork for future struggles and disappointments. In life, early triumphs and victories can be harbingers of disaster. The paucity of helpful rescue reference points in those trying moments, when something spectacular needs to happen, sow the seeds of that failure. In sports and in business, many who soared to great heights early in their careers have come crashing down with a big thud. Only a very few will reclaim their previous glory.

Young entrepreneurs who turn their ventures into gold for themselves and their partners are said to possess that Midas touch. Like Icarus, flying too close to the sun, these wunderkinds will one day find their wings damaged beyond repair by the harsh reality of future missteps and unmet challenges. Their once unobstructed path is anything but. Without those much-needed rescue reference points, they will fall with the hardest of landings. Offices on Wall Street are littered with those who lacked rescue reference points after achieving great early successes.

I am a lover of golf. It is a sport of precision and patience. The golf swing can become suddenly fickle and the thought *I got it now* quickly becomes mere conjecture. Most amateur golfers lack the mental toughness to recover from poor shots. Professional sport reveals a bitter truth of life, that those who can't rescue their game at a critical moment will crumble under pressure.

The lack of those helpful rescue reference points has particularly bedeviled pro golfers. I will focus on just two.

Jordan Spieth won major golf tournaments by the time he was only twenty-two. He was the reigning champion at the 2016 Masters. That year, he had a five-shot lead with only nine holes to go. Then he hit a bunch of poor shots and lost the tournament by three shots. At that time, he did not have rescue reference points in his mental toolbox to stop his downward slide.

Conversely, Jack Nicklaus said that had he won the 1960 US Open as an amateur he would *not* have had the success in golf because he just wouldn't have worked so hard.

Nicklaus won more major golf tournaments than anyone and came in second an astonishing nineteen times. Spieth, after years of hard work, is back in winning form.

Application to the Family

Parents need to be aware of the emotional burden their kids deal with, whether related to home life, structured activities, or by negative thinking. If the child can't deal with and handle stuff when the stakes are rather small and meaningless, they will have a hard time navigating through life when the stakes are more significant and impactful.

Instead of ignoring a bad result—often referred to as *failure*—examine what went wrong and what could have been done differently. A good beginning is for the parent to ask the child the following set of questions:

- What were you trying to accomplish?

- What happened instead?

- Why did this happen?

- What might you do differently the next time?

You can also change the pronouns and ask yourself the same set of questions. Most people skip over this impactful review and proceed to assure themselves that the outcome was not their fault. Then, they get their blame thrower out. You better start ducking.

BE SELF-AWARE

Stop the Blame Game

Too often, people refuse to find fault with themselves and blame everyone else. It's a reality of life that you will mess up. Hey, no one gets a hit at every at bat. Sometimes you will strike out, and it might happen at the worst possible time. Your job is to practice and get better. Period.

Careful conversations are required with people who believe nothing is their fault. Some alternative comments:

- "Perhaps we can examine the facts and your situation together."

- "Perhaps this point might be worthy of consideration."

- "Maybe you'll find this point equally interesting."

The problem could run deeper. It may be a good idea to uncover the cracks that currently exist in the relationship. You may need to repair the cracks first.

All company employees want to be recognized and treated as people and not cogs.

When companies refuse to understand this, they create what Tom Ziglar calls "zombies" at work. People stop dreaming of a better life and show up just for the paycheck.

The Error: "I am right," regardless of the situation, is potentially dangerous.

The Fix: Change the viewpoint and the conversation, leading to personal betterment.

If truth be told, what you refer to as "failure" only has relevance when you become a student of the event. It needs to be dissected and examined thoroughly. Once dissected and understood, learning occurs, and "failure" no longer exists.

The cleanest and clearest way to understand a loss, while maintaining pride in all that you have done, is to review your process. In time, your setbacks will become a setup for a comeback.

Contingency management includes referring to a list of your triumphs. This list provides you with instant objective evidence of things that you got right before facing the current turn of events. It is your proof that you can be as good as you think you are. It is the opposing force that prevents you from getting too down on yourself. Another question becomes a valuable tool in the discernment process: What's next?

However, you may not be equipped to ask or answer the aforementioned questions. You might believe that your capability and lack of brilliance is something you are born with.

The losing struggle of accepting failures and doing nothing about it is a heavy burden to maintain. But, once you can discard your "I'm a failure" curse you will be free to be, do, and have everything that life has to offer.

People who excel in this game of life place the target on process, execution, and next steps. The spotlight is on all the things—the moves, action, and activities—that are within their control. Because results are often subject to external factors not within one's control, the expected outcomes may not happen or can happen at some unknown point in the future. Again, I look to sport to showcase these salient points.

Our Olympic athletes show us that they can transmute doubt, loss, or hardship into a healthy outlook. These Olympic champions noted below evinced a "never give up," "I can do it" attitude. Each of their achievements is forever a part of Olympic lore. They developed the "improve upon and my time will come" attitude and mindset. These thoughts act as a springboard to future successes. The "who" you become in the moment of doubt, loss, or hardship is the consequential part of life. Becoming mentally stronger when suffering painful disappointment can enhance grit and perseverance.

Dan Jansen, the great speed skater, after many performance disappointments in succeeding Games, won a gold medal at his fourth Olympics (Lillehammer 1994). The country was riveted as he began his final 1,000 meter race. It was now or never. He won the race.

Lindsay Jacobelis, the snowboarding star, lost her lead in the final seconds of the snowboarding cross finals at her first Olympics (Turin 2006). She received the silver medal. She kept trying. In subsequent Games, she finished fifth, seventh, and fourth respectively. In intervening years, she won world championships. Sixteen years later, at her fifth Olympic Games (Beijing 2022) she was able to claim the gold prize.

Greg Louganis, considered by many to be the greatest diver who ever lived, won five gold medals in his career. The unexpected can occur at the strangest time. In the preliminary men's 3 meter springboard, while performing a reverse 2½ pike, he hit his head on the diving board. He had a concussion and his wound required stiches. Just a half hour after the incident, he was back competing. He won the gold medal in the 3 and 10 meter competition (Seoul 1988).

And I can still recall Kerri Strug's amazing vault (Atlanta 1996), which will forever remain a special highlight in Olympic history. The Russians and Romanians for decades had dominated women's gymnastics. After tearing two ligaments in her ankle on a previous vault, she was required to do just one more. This attempt would determine whether America would keep its lead and finally prevail. She landed perfectly (before collapsing in pain) to give the American gymnastics team enough points to claim the "all-around" gold medal.

Importantly, *Your Finest Hour* helps you to skip over the why bother phase of life. The why bother phase is the stage where you refuse to make the slightest effort; where you lose perspective; where your thoughts remain negative and harmful, and you just want to give up.

Turning doubt, loss, or harsdship into unwavering determination and discipline is a winning strategy in life and in sport.

Action Steps

Never repeat the same mistakes.
Find those key rescue reference points.
Let a setback be the setup for a comeback.

CHAPTER 21

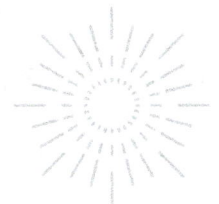

THINGS CAN ONLY GET BETTER

Innovation will shape and reshape your life.

Too many people view life as a zero-sum game: My gain is **your** loss and vice versa. These folks tend to see things as black and white, with simple rules and no room for nuance, parsing, or compromise. This rigid perspective leads to clashes between reality and one's imagined version of reality. Change is not welcomed. Individual improvement by the other is not welcomed, as such improvement may be viewed as a threat. The person refuses to accept anything that does not align with their zero-sum game beliefs that give them an advantage.

I'm here to tell you that the deficits of zero-sum thinking are significant. Zero-sum thinking protects authority while discouraging curiosity and independent thinking.

Life After Learning

Newer organizations led by forward-thinking entrepreneurs have embraced a far different approach. They value input from workers and encourage them to excel inside and outside of the company. This creates a treasured culture steeped in abundance thinking where all stakeholders prosper.

The most effective way to continue to progress through surprises and unexpected and unanticipated events is to embrace change. Depending on the circumstance, you may need to modify, innovate, adjust, and adapt your efforts.

When you refuse to modify, innovate, or adjust and adapt you will remain incapable of examining your predicament with care so you can take those important, forward-thinking next steps. This refusal is counterproductive, because, as you now know, success comes from mastering your situation.

When you focus on the thoughts and activities that are within your control, your training/opportunity/do-over days provide exponential improvement because it will also allow you to contemplate the things you should stop doing. You take a bold look at the ternary of thinking, doing, and not doing.

As entrepreneur and motivational speaker Jim Rohn has said, "Formal education will make you a living; self-education will make you a fortune."

Dealing With Relationships Is Crucial

The payoff comes in the enhancement of your important relationships. If you talk on and on about yourself, you are considered unimportant and might be tolerated. If you talk about ideas with possible answers to help others and choose to listen with intent to understand rather than with intent to be heard, you will be considered a valuable resource and perhaps a lifesaver. Talking is sharing. Listening is caring.

The payoff comes when your memorable service stands out, so your customers can easily share that your performance included "plus a little more"—and you did it on time, and did it in a professional manner.

While confidence is important, working successfully with others is the best capital in the world. Zig Ziglar believed that you build a better company by building better people. Your people get better by instilling in them the desire to improve; to develop process and expertise along the way; and to foster a life based upon continuous learning so change loses its domineering power.

Life requires constant planning. You will need to accumulate knowledge, the skills to develop more skills, and the discipline to internalize those skills until they become a part of you.

You are now ready to discover the better way to have a conversation with yourself that stops premature worry.

BE SELF-AWARE

Become a Resource

Becoming a resource to another is invaluable. Sharing articles and books you've discovered or providing news about upcoming lectures and seminars is a straightforward warm approach that demonstrates you genuinely care about prospects and customers.

Your goal is just to out-behave the competition. This becomes rather easy when you pay attention, listen, and observe. Whenever a client mentioned a grandchild or a young child, I would deliver Dr. Seuss's *Oh the Places You'll Go*. They loved that gesture. Show a genuine interested in others, and they will be genuinely interested in you.

Rather than asking, "What can I do?" you start to ask, "What should I do?" This question will also stop you from doing nothing or "just enough."

The Error: You fail to solidify personal and business relationships.

The Fix: Become an important resource to others so you remain top of mind.

Action Steps

Recognize your ability to be a resource.
Think and speak in terms of ideas and solutions.
Discard your zero-sum rules.

CHAPTER 22

THE FOREIGN LANGUAGE
OF SELF-TALK

The most important conversation you will ever have
is with yourself.

There are three distinct types of self-talk idioms: "if only," "at least," and "next time I will." "If only" is used when things do not go as planned. The regret is followed by a wish for things to be different. As in, "If only I was aware of that fact," or "If only I started this sooner," or "If only I paid more attention." This self-talk recognizes the frustration and dissatisfaction of getting close to achieving that coveted prize and carries an inherent desire to do better in the future.

When you utter, "At least," you are finding some solace in small wins, even when the outcome may not be what you had hoped for. For example, you might say, "At least, I didn't get fired," or "At least she said she'll think about going out with me," or "At least I got the last spot available." While this self-talk provides temporary comfort, it will not lead to the "If only" level of motivation.

"Next time I will" piggybacks upon the insight from the "If only" yearnings. It is here that the planning for a better outcome takes shape. One provides the switching lane for the other. It is here where self-encouragement paves the way for a different result. When you find yourself saying "If only I…," follow that up with "Next time I will…."

You will foster personal growth and better outcomes in all areas of your life. It is not just the words that count. It is the thoughts and actions backing up your sentiments that count even more.

Ingenuity

Imagine for a moment, that you are the twenty-first person waiting to be interviewed for a position you really must have. Twenty people will be interviewed before you. What can you do to improve your chances of getting the job? Here is what an enterprising young person did: He gave the secretary a note to give to the boss. The note said, "Dear Sir: I'm the 21st person in line. Don't do anything until you see me." Of course, he got the job because he thought of a way to stand out. If you want things to be different, you must be different yourself. Remember, Zig Ziglar said, "You are what you are and where you are because of what has gone into your mind. You can change what you are and where you are by changing what goes into your mind."

Today, most people believe that the chief duty of a human being is to squeeze the most out of life and achieve more than you thought you could. How would you feel if your efforts enabled you to scream to the world "I can, I will, I did." Words are not just words when they leap into your soul and strike at the heart of who you are meant to be.

Look at the word "can't." Most people have little hesitation saying, "I can't do that." Now I want you to look at how easy it becomes to do that which you thought you couldn't do. Remove the *T*. Go ahead, do it now. Imagine that you have done this. The way you removed the *T* is the way you remove an obstacle in life. It just takes imagination and effort.

When you give the ultimate effort, you are generally considered to be doing *the best you can do*. But is that enough? Your abilities and confidence would grow even more were you to do the *best that you can do plus a little more*. It's that plus a little more where going that extra mile pays huge dividends. You can provide an additional framework for others to follow when you show that deeper thinking can provide options and alternatives not available with the first level of thought.

BE SELF-AWARE

A Way to Build Your Self-Esteem

Are you internalizing the condemnation from others in thoughts like, *Look at me I can't get a break*, or *Nobody thinks I can do anything*, or *I got passed over for another promotion.*

Accordingly, a person facing such an onslaught can become jealous of others, mishandle the slightest criticism, develop insecurities, and wind up unknowingly sabotaging their own efforts.

When you are particular about who you let into your life, you are taking important steps to care for yourself and promote your own well-being. You give your life meaning and hope when you start with the thought that you will never allow another to degrade you. Then think about the learning opportunities that are available. Life is an echo. What you teach yourself makes you smarter and wiser. What you give to others you get back. Charles Dickens said, "No one is useless in this world who lightens the burden of it to anyone else."

People have gone further than they thought they could because someone else thought they could. No excuses. Give life your all.

The Error: Your poor self-image permits others to harm you further.

The Fix: Let others into your life who care for you, are kind to you, and want you to succeed.

Worry

If you are like many people, you are a worry machine. Worrying is like paying a debt you do not owe. It has been said that more people worry than work. Worry creates a high level of stress hormones that unleash soaring anxiety.

Spending too much time imagining all the calamity that is about to come crashing in around you can adversely affect you mentally and physically. It becomes a huge distraction as you obsess about your far-reaching doomsday predictions.

When you constantly worry about the future, you overlook the actions and efforts you can take today that can influence and shape your tomorrow. The future is not "predetermined" when you remain vigilant and proactive.

It is important to remember that your struggles and scars come from that which you have already experienced. And if you don't yet have the requisite experience and ability to work through the issue, you can always ask for help. You don't have to go through a new ordeal alone.

Put the Glass Down

Imagine that I am holding a glass of water in my hand.

If I were to ask you how heavy this glass of water is, what would you say?

You would offer some guesses, but they would all be irrelevant because the weight of the glass doesn't matter. What does matter is how long I choose to hold the glass of water.

If I hold it for a minute, nothing happens.

If I hold it for an hour, my arm begins to ache.

If I hold it all day, my arm would become numb and paralyzed.

The weight of the glass has not changed, but the longer I hold it the heavier it becomes.

The stresses and worries of life are like this glass of water.

If you think about it a little while, no problem.

If you think about it a little longer, it begins to hurt.

If you think about it all day long, you become paralyzed and incapable of doing anything.

Sometimes the best advice is the simplest advice: Put the glass down. Stop holding on to those worries and get on with your life. You have the tools to accomplish that.

Next, let's discover how to get the most out of your personal and business life.

Action Steps

Be conscious of the effect of self-talk.
Instead of worrying, do something about it.
Always add just "a bit more effort."

CHAPTER 23

THINK LIKE A RADICAL SAGE

Leadership is about seeing the future and setting the example.

There are three key thought principles that you want to know like the back of your hand before you can form solid relationships in your business and personal life. Do not ignore these three foundational principles:

Key Thought #1: You must be able to lead. Leadership always begins with a thought.

Key Thought #2: Look at things as they are (at work, business, and home) and then make needed changes so the situation becomes as you would like it to be. Never fight against or fail to recognize what already exists.

Key Thought #3: Rather than trying to predict the future, create it.

These three key thoughts above and the business wisdom contained below will provide you with the seeds for nurturing and hatching your life's plans. Additionally, they will stop you from thinking like a "know it all" who revels at their great idea, ignoring the fact that this idea is the only one you came up with.

When people give birth to an idea, often it is an internal signal to stop all thinking. And that is exactly what is done when you come up with that singular new idea. Effective thinking should never stop. Remember, you are looking for the best answer that effectively solves the problem, not just the best answer you could think of. Understanding this difference will save you a lot of grief and aggravation.

BE SELF-AWARE

Make Life Your Classroom

Stop thinking you can't do it. Start thinking about "small step" achievements and about which opportunities are recoverable and which are not.

Stop holding on to your regretful past. Start making "the past" the best teacher you ever had.

Stop taking out your frustrations on others. Start creating a new agenda with new priorities and do them.

Stop letting flawed self-beliefs take you in the wrong direction. Start dealing in facts and start thinking about what you want to be known for.

People may forget what you did or said. They will never forget how you made them feel. When you speak, your job is to make them feel valued.

Developing a talent is a beautiful thing. The instructions and directions you give yourself determine the extent that talent can be expressed. Courage is needed in those reclusive moments of awareness and insight.

Author John Bytheway gets to the heart of the matter when he says: "Yard by yard life is hard. Inch by inch, it's a cinch."

Keep that perspective.
The Error: You are stuck in your negative past.
The Fix: Become your personal guide into your new future.

It's time to think and behave differently. To enjoy new levels of business and personal success, you have to internalize, accept, and follow the guidelines percolating here. If you ignore these salient points, please note, that any success you have may be due to luck and chance. At some point, the uncertain future is likely to catch up with you. By then, it may be too late to save yourself.

You never, for example, want to be the turkey before Thanksgiving. Turkeys are nurtured and well-fed and, presumably, feel safest when they are most at risk. As a determined entrepreneur and lover of life, you don't want to be complacent. Success is never final, because successes have a sneaky way of making you overconfident. Whenever this happens, you can miss signs that something is awry and needs attention. And just like our turkey, when you feel the safest, you are most at risk. You won't even know that a catastrophe is lurking around the corner. In business, for example, Kodak ignored digital photography. Blockbuster ignored Netflix. What are *you* ignoring? Think about what you could also be missing in your personal and family life.

While the balance of this chapter is specific to business and entrepreneurship, think how impactful your life can be when you apply these business concepts to your personal and family life.

How to Be a True Leader

This will make your competitors very nervous.

The type of work environment you create determines how

decisions are made, how information flows, and how power is wielded. There is a big difference between a leader and a boss (here think autocratic and a *pretend leader*). The reason a wrong person could be chosen as a leader is because confidence is often mistaken for competence.

No one questions a boss. Obedience and conformity are rewarded. Workers and staff are mere followers. You do what you are told to do. If you don't follow orders, severe consequences will result. Information is retained by the privileged few. Here's the thing. Blind obedience to autocratic bosses no longer works. A boss is not a leader. A leader is never a boss.

A leader shares a vision with all who work in the company. Rules are not important because values rule the day. Information is shared with all. The liberating feeling of trust freely flows between people and groups of people, as relationships prosper. When these things happen, real communication ensues, and creativity leads to sound solutions.

A boss asks, "How do I force my workers to give me what I want?"

A leader asks, "How do I create a phenomenal work environment where everyone can flourish and even reuse their skills outside of work?"

Unlike a boss or a pretend leader, a true leader is always asking another fundamental question: "How would the person I hope to be do the thing I'm about to do?"

Leaders also look toward the future by working backward. For your customers to realize that your company should be their go-to company, your employees must always act in accordance with the company's vision and mission.

This is manifested when the default mindset coalesces around the idea this is how we do business here. You hit the mark when your customers say things like: "They make me feel important. They get it right every time. We get great value."

This, of course, is the result of great leadership.

BE SELF-AWARE

Discipline Takes You to Where You Want to Go

Life is lived first and foremost within yourself. It is here that you realize what is important and vital and what is not. You realize, to win at any cost takes little effort. Human detritus and destruction need not fill your path.

But, to win when victory can be spread among many is a testament to your skill and character. In the human development and emotional intelligence worlds, it is not what you leave *to* someone that counts, it's what you leave *in* someone that counts. A leader engages and encouarages others. A leader also values relationships and effort.

Discipline is something you do for yourself, for your team, and for your family. Your behavior firewall will never let you display behavior you would never tolerate in others. Your enduring behavior will become a far-reaching lesson that will be followed by and passed along by people both familiar and unfamiliar to you.

Because you are the framework for everything that happens in your life, your legacy provides that your kindness, caring, and mentoring will endure.

The Error: Doing the bare minimum to get by is the wrong road to take.

The Fix: When others you have taught become their better selves, and they teach others the same lesson, you have done your job well.

The Right Metrics

Only that which is measured can be controlled. Metrics let you know what is working and what is not working.

If you measure everything, you are measuring nothing. It's like doing carpet bombing when a surgical strike will do. You'll need to decide what measurements will provide you with intelligent feedback that is critical to survival and growth.

Additionally, metrics force you to re-evaluate your capabilities by looking at all the resources you have available, the processes you employ, and the priorities you give to each. Since marketing, sales, administration, and operations are components in every business you may want to know such things as: weekly revenues, receivables, and payables; amount of customer and potential customer engagements; sales commitments; cashflows; production and service capacity; customer retention, customer problems with solutions realized, etc.

In short, you need to define the problem and make sure you are focusing on the problem and not upon a symptom that may be mistaken for the problem. Next, measure the capability of the processes you have set up. By analyzing the data points you are tracking, you can confidently put the needed improvements in place.

Being Mission-Driven

A clear company vision can ensure that your enterprise is meeting the needs of the customer. Whenever company communication freely flows, its vision and mission will endure. It increases the chances that individuals are placed in positions that complement their skills. When this happens, it is more likely that the correct people will do the job right.

Think of a couple of uber-successful people whom you admire and whose traits you would like to showcase in your company. Here, for example, are a few qualities you may wish your employees and staff to follow: does the right thing; collaborative; prideful; teamwork is front and center; asking questions is more important than telling; there is no substitute for honesty; and always strive to be better.

This is by no means an all-inclusive list.

Your biggest mistake will be to assume that each person shares this vision and is ready to acknowledge the mission of the company. To reach the level of success you desire, you need to make sure that everyone is, as the saying goes, "rowing in the same direction at the desired speed." Competitive business forces are at work every day to make your company irrelevant. Only constant improvement, incessant innovation, and internalization of the company vision will keep you in the game as you beat back the competition.

Another big mistake management makes is to assume because things are *going well*, investment in customer and office relationships can now be ignored. When people feel discarded and unheard, the work and business environment can quickly turn toxic. Relationships must always be nurtured.

As an owner, you want to help your staff and employees develop the skill to grow new skills. Continually challenging your staff to be better and to do more helps them develop the capabilities to see and solve issues before they develop into big problems. Problem-solving abilities stem from experiencing varying situations. Businesses that merely tell employees and staff what to do never accomplish nearly as much as those who permit employees and staff to learn from actual experiences.

The Platinum Standard

A company can have only one Platinum Standard of Dependability. It applies within as well as externally to independent contractors and suppliers. Here's an important question to ask yourself: Will your employees, customers, and suppliers agree with your avowed standard of dependability? This idea, expressed in different ways, mirrors this same zeitgeist: *You can count on us... always. My word is our bond.* And, *if I said we will do it, it will be done every time.* When everyone in the company can freely and honestly express these types of *dependability thoughts,* you have done a wonderful job as a leader.

Even though this journey is a challenging one, you can start creating a future filled with pride, hope, and accomplishment. As you proceed down this exciting path, make these seminal principles follow you like a shadow. When you think differently, you can live differently. Your business and leadership skills will determine whether you survive and thrive.

Action Steps

Be open to new ideas.
Look for a better way.
Become disciplined.

CHAPTER 24

AN OMG MOMENT—NOW WHAT?

Values and guiding principles gain power through effort.

The companies who thrive don't do the most things. They assiduously focus upon the most *important* things.

Many companies fail in this regard.

Imagine how different things could have been had someone focused on the basics and what mattered most to their staff, employees, and customers. That is why it is critical to give particular attention to the key processes in marketing, sales, administration, and operations. This also means making it easy to do business with your company from everyone's perspective. This becomes the force multiplier, because everyone loves *easy*. To keep staff and employees energized, the values and principles of the company should promote trust and collaboration so each person can be appreciated and fully supported. To prevent customers from finding another provider, the company should understand how the customer does business, be aware of their expectations, and be able to convert them into loyal fans.

Here are a few more helpful starter questions that will assist your company to help itself with staff, employees, and customers: "What am I doing well to maintain our [employee/staff/customer] relationships?"

"How am I keeping [name the individual] phenomenally happy and satisfied?"

"What have we missed in the last conversation?"

"What must we improve to match existing expectations?"

"Have I discussed what has changed since our last conversations?"

"What threats will the industry be dealing with in the next quarter?"

When you are building expertise, in your business and personal life, the goal is to keep improving. St. Jerome said, "Good, better, best. Never let it rest. Till your good is better and your better is best."

Effort, effort, and more effort.

For a moment, let's focus on the customer. Often, when the customer is at their last straw, the company panics and invokes a false "Platinum Strategy" that they'll do better next time. Those words become just words that are out of sync with the way customers were historically treated in the past.

Your Finest Hour concepts prepare you for that next time, when a better process can prevent another subpar performance. It changes the prior poor effort into something much better and sustainable. It also reawakens the importance of always attending to the critical behavior of doing the basics well. The reality is that your changes may be too late to keep that customer who threatened to stop doing business with you active. That is the bad news. The good news is that particular poor performance will not happen again.

Lessons from the Animal World

Earlier we learned how the ant and the grasshopper taught us vastly different lessons. In this section, eagles, geese, and ants (more ants!) will show us how we can be even better than we think we can.

Eagles have sharp vision. Being watchful and observant is an essential quality for thriving in any gathering. Carefully studying the environment around you is a key first move, because it offers cues how and when to approach others. The way you look and move is more than 60 percent of one's first impression of you. Since you are not as imposing as an eagle, here are three things you can do at any gathering as you swoop in to make an impression:

1. Listen for clues as to one's preferred topic and say, "Couldn't help but overhearing that you...."

2. Listen for the mood of the conversation. Determine the tone of the conversation (e.g., serious, lighthearted, angry).

3. Mirror the last few words you heard and phrase them as a question. For example, if someone is talking about a demanding meeting they just left, mirror their last few words and ask: "The meeting was demanding?"

We like to copy each other, because it gives comfort. This can also be done with body language, tempo, vocabulary, and mood. You see these behaviors everywhere. People in conversation nodding in harmony; crossing arms and/or legs; couples walking with a bounce in their steps as their arms swing in synchrony.

BE SELF-AWARE

Teamwork Leads to Success

Imagine if your commitment was as solemn as the one made on July 4, 1776, when the signers of the Declaration of Independence "pledged to each other our lives, our fortunes, and our sacred honor."

As a society, one of the great triumphs of humanity is

to achieve something others said was impossible. Putting a man on the moon is one great example that speaks volumes about what can be achieved when people work together.

The importance and relevance of teamwork is that everyone knows something that you don't. Imagine if you can get to the point of finding joy when you discover that you do not know as much as you thought you did. Stretching your thinking may not guarantee success today, but because it guarantees learning, it could very well bring greater success tomorrow.

The effectiveness of any meeting depends on whether you show up to suspend your assumptions or show up to defend your assumptions. Every team brings its own sphere of influence where resourcefulness, creativity, and cooperation affect the production capacity of ideas. Doing the right thing and doing things right complement and balance each other. Asking this question of another can clear the path for a team's defining solution: "What evidence would we need to see to rethink this?"

The Error: You can't accomplish great things alone.

The Fix: Collaboration is a major advantage in life.

Geese teach us discipline, as they work together to fly in formation. It's the formation that permits the utmost efficiency to prevail. Their success is the ideal of teamwork and collaboration.

Teamwork also requires communication and fairness. This way people can safely swap thoughts to gain important insights. Having a mission and purpose where each member of the team lives in the world of the other is key to collaborative success.

Ants, as noted earlier, work hard. They work persistently and consistently. Success is in the struggle. It's about grit. It's about believing you can get the work done.

Your competitors would love to see you give up because you didn't do a task well on the first attempt or realize that overcoming an obstacle might take more effort than you thought. When others tell you that you do not have the intelligence or ability to do something, you have only one job. To prove them wrong!

Having the determination of grit is a choice. It's your choice to keep on trying. You may have to make more attempts. Only you can judge your improvement rate. This applies to learning new skills, changing an attitude, or creating a different strategic approach. It's about resilience and about belief in yourself. And, most importantly, it's about taking that peek into your future.

In the next chapter, watch what happens when you put these teachings together. Life begins to click.

Action Steps

Give people the attention they deserve.
Put in the effort for the results I want.
Prove my naysayers wrong.

CHAPTER 25

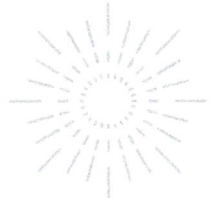

YOUR DREAMS CAN COME TRUE

Never stop dreaming.

When I was a child, television was a big influence. My friends and I alternated wanting to be Dr. Kildare (a physician), Perry Mason (a lawyer), Columbo (a homicide detective), and Mr. Novak (a high school teacher) all rolled into one. Each character had amazing qualities. Each helped find solutions to intractable problems. Each served others.

As I grew into early adulthood, those aspirations were often nowhere to be found. Fear of failing caused indifference to get the upper hand. Whenever this very young adult looked in the mirror, a stranger stared back. Harsh public ridicule throughout the adolescence years caused positive private thoughts to recede and hide deep into the canyons of my mind. Then one day, the mind reached the state of *enough* and fought back hard to get a "voice at the table."

Here is an important question to consider. How do seemingly all-powerful victim invoking private thoughts lose their influence? The answer is that the mind and the person become more positive and stronger when those thoughts change from a destructive to a boundless potential outlook. Positive, energizing

BE SELF-AWARE

Edit the Script in Your Head

The mind can swiftly change its outlook—at times, it is telling you that you are brilliant, and your peers, customers, and competitors are not. Then, just as quickly, you are reminded that you're too old, too young, too dumb, too lazy—you are just *too something*. That *too something* gives you the excuse to stop and give up.

The most difficult unaware challenge you will encounter is not that you don't know that you have a problem; it's that everyone else knows but you.

Success in this life is a matter of choice, not a matter of chance. Where the mind goes, your life is not far behind. Start by making mental reminders. You don't want to forget or misplace those key internal narratives.

In a way, adversity introduces you to yourself. You don't rise to the occasion; you fall to the level of your thinking, training, and preparation. Life is a constant search for truth and reality.

Stop thinking you are owed something by everybody. Start getting better.

Stop embracing what is not working. Start thinking efficiency.

The Error: Focusing solely on your adversities creates the untenable quicksand of life.

The Fix: Control the things you can control and let go of everything else.

thoughts used in the right way, in the right amount, and at the right time, can become very powerful and formidable.

When you embrace the three superpowers, along with the

hard work needed to upgrade your attitudes and mindsets, you will gain the competence and confidence to pursue your goals.

Your Vantage Point

Objective reality tells us that no one can do everything well. But everyone can excel at anything when their subjective reality overpowers objective reality. Remember my sport heroes in Chapter 6 who spent unimaginable time and energy, along with Herculean efforts proving others wrong.

As I noted many times before, a mistake, error, or struggle can accelerate the learning experience. Making the best out of every experience also lets you strive to become a better you.

Embracing each day as an opportunity to be better is a gift you can give yourself. When you use these days to improve, it's as if you are living for a second time, but now you are wiser.

Now you are ready to see how the power of *what if* can also help you reach your greatness.

Action Steps

Hold on to my dreams.
Improve my efforts.
There is no such thing as failing, only getting better.

CHAPTER 26

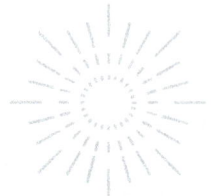

HOW FAILURE
EVOLVES INTO SUCCESS

*There is no such thing as "having failed." There is only
phenomenal progress. That's it!*

Once upon a time, failure was really looked upon as an event—
and only an event. It clocked in as a *fleeting moment in time*. It
was marked by impermanence, looked at as a mere bump in the
road. One was said *to have made a failure.*

Today, however, in the ever-escalating age of instant gratification, failure has taken on a radically different meaning. It
now leaves an indelible mark, staining the individual like an
unwanted tattoo. It has a draconian, permanent type of feel to
it. Failing has become the *end of the story*, an insidious label—as
in *you are a failure*. This label poisons the mind and follows the
individual like that proverbial shadow.

This cosmic shift in perception has caused fear (as in fear of
failing) and unhappiness to reign. It has caused people to give
up dreams, to forgo initiatives, and to worship the status quo
of life. It has provided untold millions of excuses for not getting the job done. Safety has become the new elixir. Not to try
risks nothing. Attempting to achieve could risk everything. And

today it is better to play it safe than risk attaining a new moniker of "a failure."

The Power of What If

Like confetti thrown at your favorite parade, your thoughts get thrown about and are discarded in a similar way. A thought molecule doesn't stand a chance as it becomes invisible among the masses of other thoughts. Even when a thought cries out "Here I am, I'm over here," it often goes unnoticed and unheard. The mind's endless production of fleeting ideas strips the potential life-altering power away from each proceeding thought as it struggles for recognition.

However, the mind can make a thought molecule stand out and shine, ensuring it gets the recognition it deserves. An ordinary thought can become dominant and compelling by adding the magical words *what if*. Below I offer compelling *what if* thought questions that will encourage your mind to escape an unwelcoming past while helping you achieve greatness.

What if I had thought of myself as a ten (highest number) instead of a much lower number? How much more would I have been able to achieve?

BE SELF-AWARE

Create Your Life

Life is often lived upside down and inside out, full of differing interpretations, perspectives, and twists and turns. You cherish those tangible things that others can see. But those things can be fleeting and transitory at best. You disparage those intangible thoughts that remain invisible to all but you. Yet, they can be enduring and long-lived.

Who you become is the driver of a successful life. Clarity of thought becomes extremely important. You learn what thoughts and actions need to go and which ones need to stay and be improved upon. It's like Leonardo da Vinci chiseling away at a statue. When enough of the pieces that add nothing to the masterpiece are removed, he was left, like you, with a masterpiece.

The Error: You pay attention to the tangible and the fleeting so you can show off to others.

The Fix: You have the power to create the person who you want to become. Now go do it.

What if I had looked at the proverbial glass as half full rather than half empty? How much more would I have been able to achieve?

What if I had differentiated mere opinion from wise counsel? How much more would I have been able to achieve?

What if I had taken into account the sway my emotional state had over my decision making? How much more would I have been able to achieve?

What if I had believed in myself, even when others voiced a contrary opinion? How much more would I have been able to achieve?

What if had expressed my sincere gratitude to those who truly cared about my success? How much more would I have been able to achieve?

What if I had realized that I am the only one in charge of me? How much more would I have been able to achieve?

What if I had fallen in love with my future earlier? How much more would I have been able to achieve?

What if I were now able to handle the chaos in my life with greater clarity and skill? How much more would I have been able to achieve?

What if I had become aware that taking the path of least

resistance in and of itself is not a strategy? How much more would I have been able to achieve?

What if I had understood that terrible things don't happen on their own, that I had provided a helping hand? How much more would I have been able to achieve?

What if I had recognized that it was more beneficial to have timely completed that task rather than continued to procrastinate? How much more would I have been able to achieve?

What if I had become aware that I slowed my forward progress when I overvalued the talents of others and undervalued my special gifts? How much more would I have been able to achieve?

What if I had not believed that everyone was smarter than me and hadn't given in and given up at every opportunity? How much more would I have been able to achieve?

What if I had understood that what happens in reality pales to what happens within my mind? How much more would I have been able to achieve?

BE SELF-AWARE

Graciousness

When you lead by example you can lead yourself and others.

You tap into the "giving feeling" because it grounds you.

You see the good in others.

Kindness allows you to do your job effectively and to get things done.

The true measure of a person lies in how he treats someone who can do him no good. Some people help others only if they can also gain from the situation. And then there are people who focus upon how they can be of service to others.

Leaders mightily advance the goodness in their community

while those non-leaders advance themselves and, in so doing, miss opportunities for greatness.

The Error: Thinking you need situational power and authority to lead.

The Fix: Leading because you see a need and opportunity to assist others.

What if I had focused on the fact that *if it is to be it is up to me* and realized that it is impossible to remain stagnant and still accomplish goals? How much more would I have been able to achieve?

The answer to each question is: You would have achieved *a lot* more. But here is your new master thought: It is never too late.

Author Napoleon Hill said it best in *Think and Grow Rich:* "More gold has been mined from the mind of men than the earth itself." These thoughts will help you mine more of your value than you ever imagined.

Action Steps

Never consider myself a failure.
My thoughts will take me toward my goals and destinations.
Energize my thoughts with "what if" questions.

CHAPTER 27

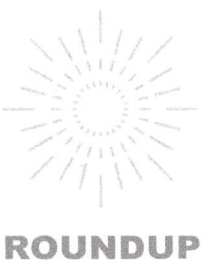

ROUNDUP

It's those small thought molecules that pack the most power.

As you have already seen, your three superpowers are there if you chose to activate them. Your superpowers of appropriate response, awareness, and thought creation and thinking control can prevent regrettable words from gushing forth when dealing with people who irritate you, rub you the wrong way, or are the subject of your frustration for annoying transgressions. Your superpowers can keep the "wrong words" from making the situation worse. Yet, many people make things worse. Their instant reaction begs broader questions: Why overreact at all? Is it not better to break the cycle of overreaction? It is important to differentiate between an inappropriate overreaction and an appropriate constructive response. In the former, the relationship could be damaged beyond repair. In the later, a mutual understanding is forged that can heal the relationship.

When you overreact to someone's intentional or unintentional poor choice of words, devious put downs, or thoughtless speech or actions, you are complicit. You share blame for further igniting the flames of discord that caused the imbroglio. While it is true that you have the power to overreact or not, relationship ashes are evidence of this destructive force when you do. But here is the thing: You have the power to prevent the coming conflagration.

BE SELF-AWARE

Let Mutual Challenges Unite Us

Each of us is similar because we emerge from the womb with a cry for help and exit this life with a whisper. Because at some point, we will face "unfair" headwinds of life. Because we suffer before it is necessary and, often, more than is necessary. Because we have a range of emotions and use them at the wrong time. Because adversity lays down an "insurmountable" challenge that is often winnable. Because we complain a lot and do little. Because we feel we can't adapt and excel. Because when we don't give meaning and purpose to our lives, we create the wrong kind of outcomes.

The Error: You believe you have little in common with other people and unnecessarily enter battle mode.

The Fix: Realize that we all want the same things and we're more likely to achieve them together.

Awareness about how to respond, while subduing the volcanic urge to erupt, is life-changing. No longer would you be so self-destructive. No longer would you maintain your victim consciousness.

In the end, all of life's drama becomes so irrelevant, silly, senseless, and banal. A total waste of energy and time. For many, jumping to conclusions is a way of life that ignites those flames of emotions. We will all eventually wind up in the same state: dead. Therefore, while we can, doesn't it make sense to embrace life, to enhance relationships, and call a truce to the harm we cause others?

How to Reclaim Your Life

Your superpowers can also be used as a protective device when you have a conversation with yourself. What you say and how you respond to your internal conversations is also rather important. When you slander yourself, it is difficult to escape the ingrained perceptions from your past. It is not an uncommon thought to believe yourself to be too stupid to advance in your job, for example.

When you continue to slander yourself, you also become a victim. Out of necessity, the mind tries to protect you by blaming others for your current situation. This frees you from doing anything constructive to make the situation better. This is a pretty neat trick the mind plays. It is so much easier to blame your boss, your coworkers, your spouse, your in-laws—anyone but yourself.

Committing slander against yourself is the first step. Blaming others is the second step. Empowering that which is false and not helpful (your slander) over that which is true and helpful (you are better than you think) enables you to weave a fictional story that permits the blame game to continue unabated.

Remember: You're Better Than This

When your self-confidence wavers, it is always a potent idea to pull out that confidence letter you wrote to yourself (see Chapter 10). Paragraph one is congratulatory; it reminds you of all the highlights of your life to this point in time. Update it continually, and pull it out when you need a reminder of all the times you did well and were proud of yourself. (If you do not have a confidence letter, create it now.)

Paragraph two of that letter looks three years into the future and reflects on all that you have accomplished over that period of time. You will review and praise yourself on how you have changed as a person. This section could include how your thinking works *for* you, and no longer *against* you. You can talk about how you were very negative and fearful. Now the opposite is true. You can talk about how you tiptoed through life treading carefully so you wouldn't make a mistake; now mistakes are moments of insights that have led to great imagination and accomplishment. Talk about those accomplishments. The lack of self-confidence no longer defines you. You know one of two things will happen with any experience: You either will have accomplishments and achievements, or you will learn something. Wisdom becomes the square root of your experiences. Therefore, the more you attempt, the wiser you become.

Remember, it's your life. Solving life's problems is an awesome responsibility. Try a different approach to alleviate your current stress level and take back your self-esteem and self-confidence.

BE SELF-AWARE

The Secrets That Are Secrets No More

Here are fifteen things you can do right now to change your life:

1. Never retaliate or seek revenge.

2. Get more out of life by giving first.

3. Beware of your comfort zone and path of least resistance.

4. Always give sincere praise when due.

5. Always consider differing viewpoints.

6. Determine the degree of responsibility you should shoulder for events that happen.

7. Words are a weapon of choice; what is said can't be unsaid.

8. The best self-talk is the conversation that leads to "next time I will" thinking.

9. People are not mind readers; make sure they know how grateful you are.

10. There is real power in thinking things through without anger.

11. Know what an ideal outcome looks like and what has to be true when the project is finished.

12. Never confuse legality (what you can do) with morality (what you should do).

13. Mistakes are the important messengers of life.

14. Doubt what you know. Be curious about what you don't know. Update your information.

15. Be known as the person who gets the job done.

The Error: Being unfocused and unclear gets in the way of sound decision making.

The Fix: Create both to-do and not-to-do lists.

Better Decision Making

To enhance any move that you make remember to:

- **Look at the facts.** Jumping to conclusions only leads to unpreparedness and shock when things don't work out as intended. Discard what you have taken for granted that is no longer true.

- **Ask questions**. Here's a great one: "What would have to be true for this decision to be the best one for me right now?"

- **Gather information.** Then, in an unbiased manner, consider different ways (perspectives) to apply the information to your current situation.

It is also important to be comfortable with change and to make sure that any adaptations, shifts, and adjustments work for you. You may also wish to consider the following:

1. Dealing with change takes time, and you will not live forever.

2. Only you have the power to change how things are. The way you are today has nothing to do with the way you can be tomorrow. You can change how you think about things, take enlightened actions, and replace bad habits with good habits.

3. You cannot change other people. But when you change, other people will respond to those changes. This is the humanness factor at play.

4. Change, like life, is hard. But change with understanding and perseverance is achieveable.

5. Change is the immutable rule of life. If you forget this rule, you will always be fighting a losing battle.

It   is now time to free yourself from your self-imposed shackles and live the life you were meant to live. Don't let fate have the last word. This book is your lifetime refresher course that you will pick up time and time again. You have read about and discovered a reservoir of life-changing principles, thoughts, ideas, and concepts. Instead of living with just potential and possibilities on the horizon, your newfound courage will permit you to change your life into a reality of your own making. Your life and your future are in your hands. And your finest hour is closer than you think.

Action Steps

Write my confidence letter today.
Recognize the urgency of now.
Combine thought with action to make things possible.

At the beginning of this work, you probably had a lot of unanswered questions. The weak and the strong; the vulnerable and the secure; the ineffectual and the capable are musing over the same questions. They range from "Is this really for me?" to "How will I handle taking two steps back to my one meager step forward?" As is the case with trying anything new, there is a period of adjustment and evaluation. The old you would have summarily discounted trying something different. The new you is now willing to venture a bit into the unknown. The saga of your story, when you give it serious consideration, is a complex weave of textured thought. On the one hand, it is hampered by stinging adversities, yet buoyed by upbeat possibilities, waiting to be turned into triumphs.

Remember, if nothing changes, nothing changes. After getting this far with your reading, do you really want nothing to change?

You now possess an effective way to detox your life. Cleaning out the bad stuff that hindered your progress is a mighty first step. Making room for the unfamiliar new stuff is important. Using it is even more important.

The internal life you nurture determines the outer life you lead. The Learning Mode Effect treasures feedback and course corrections. This conquering doublet will always improve the internal life faster than anything else known to mankind.

The buzz word for years has been *moderation.* Because life is fragile, and you don't know how close you are to "the end," you can't afford to improve with a ho-hum, lazy, moderate effort. You can't move at a balanced and moderate pace. No. It's your life. So, you must pick up the pace with all deliberate speed. There is a definite weighty degree of urgency.

While the principles discussed herein may solve or ameliorate your most pressing problems, the goal and intention of this book is to give you the tools to transform your life—so you can get the most out of life—every day. Now it's your turn to show life what you got! And it is also your turn to prove others wrong. Just don't wait too long.

WHAT DOES YOUR NAME STAND FOR?

Crack the name code for your greatness to be recognized.

This is a great exercise to pass down to your family. It gets all the members thinking about the values they would want associated with their name. The kids and grandkids always have fun with this. I'll use my last name as the acrostic. The kids and grand-kids will come up with alternative options, which is fantastic. The important thing is that the family feels really good about this exercise. The parents explain why each selection is especially important to them. Haber as an acrostic looks like this:

Hopeful nature
Accountable for actions
Bulldozing through obstacles
Encourages others
Re-inventing the self as you evolve and become wiser and older

H

Hope is a noun—not a word that is used as a verb. Why? Because you can't *hope* something to happen without effort on your part. However, a Haber can improve skills by employing a consistent effort and, therefore, have hope.

A

Accountability is the first rule of growth. A Haber blooms into something wonderful when they are responsible for their actions.

B

Bulldozing through obstacles gets us to necessary solutions. Each day we will face challenges, also called obstacles. A Haber does not focus on a problem and give in. A Haber focuses on solutions and overcomes.

E

Encourages, engages, and supports lasting relationships. When you encourage and support peers, family, and friends, relationships flourish. Therefore, a Haber engages with and encourages others.

R

Re-inventing persona is the way a Haber evolves. Things change all the time. There is an old saying, "If you are through changing, you are through." A Haber knows that life requires evolving and re-inventing.

THE SEVEN KEY WORDS YOU SHOULD NEVER FORGET

Great relationships are like great tailoring:
The stronger the stitch the longer it lasts. You are
learning how to make a stronger stitch.

Wouldn't it be something if you were referred to as *The Greatest.* Wouldn't you like to be known as the Greatest Employer in the World? What about the Greatest Friend in the World? How about the Greatest Spouse in the World? The Greatest Parent in the World? The Greatest Child in the World?

The surest way to improve how others feel about you is to understand what is needed of you in the moment and provide it. The next best way is to sincerely apologize. Consider saying these seven words: "I'm sorry. I apologize. Please forgive me."

Have you ever wanted to take someone by the shoulders, shake them, and say, "You're doing it again." This feeling is common when repeated bad behavior is part of one's répertoire. Below I have noted some examples of reprehensible behavior. Perhaps you'll even recognize yourself.

Do you remember a time when you were in a business meeting and took all the credit for a colleague's idea?

Do you remember a time in a social gathering when you openly and rudely chastised your friend for espousing an idea you disagreed with?

Do you remember a time when you embarrassed your child in front of their friends? (Well, they never forgot.)

Do you remember a time your spouse warned you, to no avail, not to tell that funny story because she wanted to tell it that evening? (And you told it anyway.)

Your default reaction of excuse making only drives the stake of disapproval that much deeper.

However, these seven magic words are the balm that can soothe the hurt. So, the next time you find yourself in one of those uncomfortable situations when people are looking at you funny or shaking their heads disapprovingly, say in a meaningful and sincere way, "I'm sorry. I apologize. Please forgive me." Peace and calm might be restored. The "might" is a warning that your integrity may not be the symbol of perfection that you think it is. Your integrity's bright lights may be dimmed by other poor behavior.

APPENDIX C

THREE KEY COMPONENTS FOR SUCCESSFUL CONVERSATIONS

The conversation is the relationship.

I remember the time that my wife and I were homeward bound after enjoying a wonderful vacation. All that stood between us and home was the distasteful task of locating our luggage on carousel 6. As the sea of people around the carousel evaporated, we continued to wait. The luggage never came. Hope turned into despair when the steady hum of the conveyor belt stopped.

Immediately we headed toward the Lost & Found office which was located off to the side of the baggage claim area. We saw it right away. The blue ribbons tied around each handle made it easy to find. Inexplicably our luggage had been placed on an earlier flight.

Upon arriving home, a thought popped into my mind: *If one goes to a lost and found when something is lost, where does a person go when they have lost their way?* When a person becomes mentally lost and confused about who they are and what to do about it, they don't say, "Have you seen me? I'm lost." A lost and found is for things, not for humans. Silly, you say. Well, it's really not so silly.

Day in and day out, people refuse to *learn* from new

experiences. They reframe mistakes in the worst demeaning way. They remain stuck in the reality of their choosing and are incapable of creating a better life for themselves. They are just drowning in that familiar stinkin' thinkin' thought pattern.

Your Finest Hour teaches how to live more effectively, while thinking differently. It is your personal lost and found.

Here are some thought-provoking questions you may wish to consider right now. You may have noticed similar questions in other chapters.

Is my integrity on full display?

What was I placed on this earth to do?

What is my #1 must-get-done goal for the day?

What are my peers and colleagues really saying about me that would shock me?

If I continue on my current path, will my life improve or deteriorate one year from now?

If I could learn something new that would benefit me the most, what would that be?

What is my primary "job" in this particular situation?

What assumptions are getting in the way of thinking things through?

Is my perspective the only way to look at what happened?

Understanding that others are willing to offer help and support is an incredibly freeing experience. Think of all the times when you felt that you had no one to turn to for guidance. Remember how lost, isolated, and disheartened you felt? Often the road to abject despair is paved with a singular weighty two-part thought: *That I should be able to solve all my problems quickly and efficiently and that I should be able to have all the answers to my salient questions.*

The tumult of living life causes you to forget a primal fact: For years, your family answered your questions, large or small, significant or insignificant, until you were old enough to leave home. You had the comfort of leaning upon the problem-solving wisdom of others.

Do you think that being an adult means you become omnipotent and omniscient and you have all the answers? One day you're receiving help as a youngster. And another day, as an adult, society expects that you know it all. Absurd, but sadly true. With all of society's pressure, it is difficult to admit you just won't ever know it all.

Navigating a new path with lessons learned can be the greatest gift of all.

Discovering that it is prudent to ask for "directions" when you have lost your way is significant. A great day approaches as you correct your coordinates.

Despair will give way to joy as you discover, with the help of others, that additional options and answers can also be explored because you chose not to go it alone.

It's Always the Conversation

Exploration of your map of life is always accompanied by conversations. Conversations can erect barriers that block respectful and meaningful relationships from developing. Or conversations can create lasting, respectful connections that permit collective thoughts and feelings to be heard and considered. The quality of the conversation keeps relationships moving in one direction or another.

Three conversational elements discussed here have the potential to take relationships to a deeper, more fulfilling level of caring and understanding. Conversations are like a friendly tennis match: I hit the ball to you, and you hit it back to me. Here, instead of a ball, it's the conversation. This conversation volley keeps the relationship strong and the understanding clear.

Conversation component 1.
And the next step will be?

Conversation component 2.
What makes you say that?

Conversation component 3.
Before making a final decision, let's review to make
sure it works.

And the Next Step Will Be?

Too many people leave a conversation thinking everything is fine. Except it is not fine. Uncertainty reigns because people are unsure of the next steps that must be pursued. Usually, there is always a next step: A call to be made, paperwork to fill out, a question to be answered, more research to be done, another meeting to set up, a conclusion and decision to be finalized and approved. The *next step component* creates certainty for subsequent activity that needs to be considered. It creates a blueprint for what still needs to be done, by whom and when, along with the next steps to be followed. Accordingly, it is necessary to review who is on your side, who you want on your side, and who no longer should be on your side.

What Makes You Say That?

Understanding what is being said often requires an inquiry into your own perspective. How you see things becomes important.

It will affect how the issue at hand should be examined and what action should be taken to fix or eliminate it. Examining the issue places the spotlight on possible blind spots. For example, this inquiry may uncover the trust level people have about the pending decision, pinpoint unacknowledged challenges, or reveal key information yet to be reported. A deep dive into this query could also divulge the degree of harmony and disagreement that exists, as the issue at hand is further explored.

Before Making a Final Decision, Let's Review to Make Sure It Works

Often negotiations are about competing positions, like *I win, you lose.* Ideally, they should be about *win-win*—in other words, everyone got what was important to them.

Negotiations that are of the *win-lose* (competitive), *lose-win* (avoidance), or *lose-lose* (compromise) variety leaves unhappiness in their wake. It's a great idea before making a final decision if facts and impending consequences (long- and short-term) can be reviewed and discussed along with the possible aftereffects. It is also important to examine what you are thinking but not saying and what has changed since you last broached this subject.

• • •

These components are also vital to use when clarity of thought and action are required. Whether you are searching for facts, wish to understand something new, need to overcome a challenge, or improve upon the status quo, these conversation components will serve you well. Knowing what needs to happen next, what the other person is thinking, and reviewing the major points discussed goes a long way to making sure everyone is on the same page and willing to proceed. Gaining essential and far-reaching information as you travel in the right direction is invaluable.

Always confirm next steps and reasons why a person says what they say, and then review the terms of the deal again before making that final decision. This conversational trifecta will help you make better decions each and every time.

APPENDIX D

SEVEN ESSENTIAL QUESTIONS TO USE IN FRAUGHT TIMES

Without a beginning there can be no end.

In rational times, it was fair to say that you were right when your facts were right. Today some can't even stipulate to the same set of facts. Consequently, people insist their facts are right when their facts are actually wrong. Truth is no longer truth.

Because communication between people is as important as water is to a plant, being right when you are wrong cannot be sustainable. Fixating on who is right and who is wrong is the incorrect inquiry. Rather, it is best to ask, "How are we going to get through this together, so it works for each of us?" It is critical to make business and personal relationships work simply because you are involved in them. Making failed relationships work again is what keeps people up at night. You can live in the land of hope and pray that relationships somehow resolve themselves and, in the meantime, you can continue to remain frustrated, upset, and anxious. Nothing will be different, and you will remain in your sorry state. Or, you can attempt to engage the other in conversation. Making the first move doesn't guaranty success. It's just a start. The cliché that it takes two to tango is true when you try to improve a relationship. You may want to engage the other with any one of these questions to get a dialogue started.

- What is the most important thing we should be talking about?

- What matters most to you?

- From your viewpoint, how did I contribute to this mess?

- I like to imagine recreating our "old" times together—what would we have to do to make this happen?

- Can you help me understand how the "best relationship" turned out this way?

- What can we do as a first step toward reconciliation?

- What else?

SOURCES

Abbott, Jim and Brown, Tim. *Imperfect: An Improbable Life.* Ballantine Books, 2012.

Bogues, Tyrone and Utti, Jacob. *Muggsy: My Life From a Kid in the Projects to the Godfather of Small Ball.* Triumph Books, 2022.

Chernow, Ron with Grover Gardner. *Titan: The Life of John D. Rockefeller, Sr.* Random House, 1998.

Christensen, Clayton M., Allworth, James and Dillon, Karen. *How Will You Measure Your Life?* Harper Business Review Classic, 2017.

Coyle, Daniel. *The Talent Code: Greatness Isn't Born. It's Grown. Here's How.* Bantam Books, 2009.

Dalio, Ray. *Principles*, Avid Reader Press, 2017

Emerson, Kim. "Put the Glass Down" (video). YouTube.

Frankl, Viktor E. *Man's Search for Meaning.* Beacon Press: 1959, rev. 2014.

Friedman, Thomas L. *Thank You for Being Late: An Optimist's Guide to Thriving in the Age of Accelerations.* Macmillan, 2016.

Gladwell, Malcom. *David and Goliath: Underdogs, Misfits, and the Art of Battling Giants.* Little Brown and Company, 2013.

Grant, Adam. *Hidden Potential: The Science of Achieving Greater Things.* Penguin Random House, 2023.

Grant, Adam. *Originals: How Non-Conformists Move the World.* Penguin Books, 2017.

Grant, Adam. *Think Again: The Power of Knowing What You Don't Know*. Penguin Random House, 2021.

Greenfield, Martin with Hall, Wynton. *Measure of a Man-From Auschwitz Survivor to Presidents' Tailor.* Regnery Publishing, 2014.

Hardy, Darren. *The Compound Effect: Jumpstart Your Income, Your Life, Your Success*. Vanguard Press, 2020.

Hasan, Medhi. *Win Every Argument: The Art of Debating, Persuading, and Public Speaking*. Henry Holt & Company, 2023.

Heath, Chip and Heath, Dan. *Decisive: How to Make Better Choices in Life and Work*. Random House Audio, 2013.

Hill, Napoleon. *Think and Grow Rich*. Napoleon Hill Foundation, 2019.

Marden, Orison Swett. *Every Man A King: How to Control Thought and Exercise the Power of Self-Faith over Others*. Musaicum Books, 2017.

Marquardt, Michael J. and Tiede, Bob. *Leading with Questions: How Leaders Discover Powerful Answers by Knowing How and What to Ask. 3rd Edition* John Wiley and Sons, 2023.

Moss, Caroline. "This Ad from 1926 Is the Driving Force Behind Much of the Internet's Viral Content." Business Insider, Dec. 2, 2013.

Nightingale, Earl. *The Strangest Secret*. Merchant Books, 2013.

Pink, Daniel H. *Power of Regrets*. Riverhead Books, 2022.

Schaefer, PhD, Dan. *Click! The Competitive Edge™ for Sports, Entertainment, and Business*. Peak Performance Strategies® LLC, 2012.

Sobel, Andrew and Panas, Jerold. *Power Questions: Build Relationships, Win New Business, and Influence Others.* Wiley, 2012.

Taleb, Nassim Nicholas. *The Black Swan: The Impact of the Highly Improbable.* Penguin Random House, 2010.

Wancho, Tom. "Tom Dempsey's Kicking Shoe." Bullock Museum. Accessed 2016. https://www.thestoryoftexas.com/discover/artifacts/tom-dempsey-shoe-spotlight-092515.

Ziglar, Tom. *Choose to Win: Transform Your Life One Simple Choice at a Time.* Nelson Books, 2019.

Ziglar, Zig. with Ziglar, Tom. *Born to Win: Find Your Success Code.* Prabhat Prakashan, 2016.

Ziglar, Zig. *Secrets of Closing the Sale.* Revell, 1984, rev. 2003.

Ziglar, Zig. *See You at the Top.* Pelican Publishing, 1975, rev. 2005.

ABOUT THE AUTHOR

DENNIS HABER

Dennis is an attorney who found his true calling and purpose in life helping others achieve for themselves what they never thought they could do. He is among the relatively few Ziglar Legacy Certified trainers and coaches in the world. He is also a prolific writer. *Don't Play with Fire: How to Keep Your Greatness from Going Up in Flames* was his seminal book in the human development/ self-help field. He is also the author of *Piggy Bank Your Home: Tap into the Power of Reverse Mortgages* and coauthor of *The Secret Power Behind Real Estate Donations* with Chase Magnuson. He has been a contributing author to books on personal, business development, and legal issues, including *Happily Ever After... Expert Advice for Achieving the Retirement of Your Dreams; CPA's Guide to Long-Term Care Planning; Momentum;* and *The Fearless Entrepreneurs.* His articles have appeared in many legal publications, including the prestigious *New York Law Journal.*

Dennis has created multiple platforms for further exploration of the bedrock principles found in this book:

e-Workbook. Continue on your journey toward greatness with these materials on dennishaber.com.

Keynote speaking. Let Dennis show you how to squash, extinguish, and trample upon those high-volume negative thoughts so they no longer have the power to stop, restrain, and halt your progress through life. He shows how to once and for all take control over your life so you are respected and loved by others in your life.

Individualized coaching. Your journey to become *life's learning master* begins with a customized package that knocks fear out of your way so you can get anywhere you want to go in life. Our co-creative process helps you to identify untapped potential, along with skills and capabilities that need to be fully developed.

Workshops. Hosted at corporate headquarters and community centers, workshops provide communal, reciprocal, and interactive experience that provides immediate feedback.

For more information, please visit dennishaber.com.

Contact Dennis at Dennis@DennisHaber.com.

www.ingramcontent.com/pod-product-compliance
Lightning Source LLC
Chambersburg PA
CBHW060514130626
46553CB00002B/492